SPECTRUM

Writing

Grade 3

Spectrum®

An imprint of Carson-Dellosa Publishing LLC
Greensboro, North Carolina

Spectrum®
An imprint of Carson-Dellosa Publishing LLC
P.O. Box 35665
Greensboro, NC 27425 USA

11-175137811

Table of Contents Grade 3

Chapter 1 Focusing on Main Ideas

Chapter 2 Organizing Ideas

Chapter 3 Writing Your Own Thoughts

Chapter 4 Writing to Inform or Explain

Table of Contents, continued

Chapter 5 Writing to Describe

Chapter 6 Writing to Entertain

NAME _____

Look at the picture. What do you see?

Playing games with your family is fun.

One picture can tell many things. If you look at the whole picture, though, it has one big, or main, idea. The sentence under the picture tells the main idea of the picture.

Now, look at this picture. Circle the sentence below that states the main idea of the picture.

Everyone loves the desert.

Animals and plants live in the desert.

Nothing is alive in the desert.

Lesson 1 See the Main Idea

Here is another picture. Write a sentence that states the main idea of the picture.

Main idea: _____

_____

_____

_____

Draw a picture in the space below. What is your picture about? Write the main idea of your picture on the line.

Main idea: _____

_____

On Your Own

Making a scrapbook is a fun activity. It is also a good way to save family pictures and memories. Get permission to use some family photos. Glue them on construction paper or a scrapbook page. For each photo, write a sentence that states the main idea.

Lesson 2 Add a Title

The title of a story tells what the story is about. What is each picture about?
Circle the best title.

Keeping Busy

Out for a Walk

Alex's Bad Day

Building for Tomorrow

Time Goes By

City Plans New Park

Vacation Ideas

School Days Return

"Share Your Pet" Day

Lesson 2 Add a Title

Write a title for each picture.

_____
_____

_____
_____

_____
_____

Lesson 3 Name a Story

The title of a story tells what the story is about. Read each story. Then, answer the question.

Molly has a problem. Her pet turtle will not stay in its box. Every day, it gets out. Mom does not like to find a turtle in the hallway or the bathroom. What can Molly do?

Molly goes for a walk in the back yard. She sees Andy playing in his kiddie pool in the next yard. Molly has an idea. She gets an okay from Mom, then starts to work. Molly puts some water in her old kiddie pool. Then, Mom helps her put some big rocks in the pool. Finally, Molly puts her turtle in. He looks right at home.

What is the best title for this story? Circle your choice.

Pets Are Hard Work   A New Home for Turtle   Molly and Mom

It was raining. Jake couldn't believe it. He had wanted to play outside all day today. He sat and watched the water drip down the window.

Jake got some crayons and started to draw a picture. He drew himself playing outside. He showed blue sky and a shining sun. Jake worked hard at his picture. When he finally looked up, he couldn't believe it. The view out the window looked just like his picture!

What is the best title for this story? Circle your choice.

A Weather Report   Jake's Very Bad Day   Rainy Day Drawing

Lesson 3 Write a Title

Read each story and write a title on the line. Remember that most words in a title begin with a capital letter. Only words such as *a, and,* and *the* are not capitalized. Also, the first and last word of a title are always capitalized.

_____

Hanna had been looking forward to this day all week. It was "Dads and Daughters" day at school. She laughed as her dad tried to squeeze into her desk chair. Dad was glad when Hanna offered him a bigger chair.

After morning meeting, Hanna had a big surprise. The teacher called her up to the author's chair. She got settled, then she began reading a story. It was a special story that she had written about her dad. Hanna's dad smiled. He had been looking forward to this day all week, too.

_____

The wind tugged at Shawn's jacket and made his hair stand up straight. It was so windy that Shawn's buddies had given up on their baseball game. The pitchers couldn't get the ball anywhere near the batters. Now what could they do?

The guys were all sitting on the bleachers when a plastic bag went rolling along the ground. That gave Shawn an idea. He ran home for some grocery bags and string.

Back at the ball field, it didn't take long to tie a long string to the handles of a grocery bag. Shawn let go of the bag and up it went. It puffed up with air and bounced on the wind. Pretty soon there were a dozen fat white kites up in the air. Shawn thought it was a good ending to a sad baseball game.

Lesson 4 Find the Main Idea

The main idea of a paragraph is what the paragraph is all about.

Read the paragraph and decide what it is about. Then, circle your choice below.

Which game is older, basketball or football? Both of these games are more than 100 years old, but football, as we know it, got started about 15 years before basketball did. Soccer beats both of them, however. Soccer rules were first published in 1863, about 12 years before football's first game took place.

Football is older than basketball.

Soccer is the oldest game of all the sporting events.

The games we play have been around for many years.

Now, read this paragraph. What is its main idea? Circle your choice below.

I was up before 6 o'clock. I washed up and got dressed. Then, I set out breakfast for the whole family. By the time they got up, I had already eaten. I brushed my teeth and put my backpack on. Then, I sat on the front step. It was the first day of school, and the bus would not come for another hour.

I got ready for school early.

I made breakfast for my family.

I always brush my teeth after breakfast.

Lesson 4 Find the Main Idea

Read each paragraph. Then, answer the question.

> Snakes are interesting animals. They do not have any legs, so they move around by wiggling their entire body. They also do not have eyelids, so their eyes are always open. Most snakes can also swallow things that are bigger than its head. These features and more make snakes interesting animals.

What is the paragraph's main idea? Write it in a sentence.

_____

_____

> Getting lost in a crowd can be frightening. It is only natural for a child to want to look around for the person he or she was with. But wandering around is not safe. The child should stay in one place and wait. That way, the parents will be able to find the child. Parents should teach this as early as possible.

What is the paragraph's main idea? Write it in a sentence.

_____

_____

Lesson 5 Build Sentences and Paragraphs

You know all of these things about sentences.

- A sentence is a group of words that tells a complete thought.

- A sentence always begins with a capital letter.

- A sentence always ends with an end mark—either a period, a question mark, or an exclamation point.

When writers put sentences together in a group, it is called a paragraph. A **paragraph** tells about one topic. Read this paragraph about ferrets.

> I do not think ferrets are good pets. Ferrets cost more than other small pets, such as hamsters, gerbils, or even rabbits. They require quite a large cage, which is also costly. All small pets make messes, but ferrets are messier and smellier than most. Ferrets also chew on things and may cause harm both to themselves and to the things they chew on. For these reasons, ferrets do not make good pets.

Notice that all of the sentences are about the same subject: ferrets as pets. All of the sentences begin and end correctly. Also, notice that the first sentence is pushed in, or indented. Whenever you write a paragraph, you must indent the first sentence.

Read the paragraph, below. The paragraph contains two errors. Find and circle them.

> Hamsters are perfect pets. They do not cost very much, and they require a fairly small cage My mom likes the fact that they are quiet. I like the fact that I feed them once a day and clean their cage once a week. best of all, it is fun to watch hamsters play in their tunnels.

Lesson 5 Build Sentences and Paragraphs

What is your favorite kind of pet? It might be a
pet you have or a pet you would like to have.
Complete this sentence.

My favorite kind of pet is _____.

Write a paragraph about that kind of pet. When you finish writing, ask
yourself the questions at the bottom of the page. Make any corrections
that you need to.

_____

_____

_____

_____

_____

_____

_____

_____

_____

_____

Questions to Ask About a Paragraph

Does each sentence begin with a capital letter?
Does each sentence end with an end mark?
Is the first sentence of the paragraph indented?
Does the paragraph tell about just one topic?

Lesson 5 Build Sentences and Paragraphs

Have you ever dreamed about having a wild kind of a pet? I mean a really crazy pet. It might be a dinosaur, a dragon, or a dog-headed lion! Write a paragraph about this kind of a pet. Tell why it would or would not be a good pet to have.

_____

_____

_____

_____

_____

_____

_____

_____

_____

_____

_____

_____

_____

Now that you are finished writing, look back at the Questions to Ask About a Paragraph on page 14 to check your paragraph.

Lesson 6 Stay on Topic

When you write a paragraph, write about just one thing at a time. If you stay on topic, your writing will be more clear and more interesting.

Paco wrote about planting a tree. Read Paco's paragraph.

> There is a new park at the end of the block. We planted an oak tree there last week. First, we had to dig a big hole. Mr. Orez put in some special soil. Then, it took three of us to move the tree into the hole. It was heavy! We all scooped the dirt back around the tree. Then, Mr. Orez taught us a goofy dance. When I was little, I took dancing lessons. He said it would pack the soil down so the tree could stand up. It must have worked. The tree looks great.

Paco did a good job with his paragraph. His ideas are clear, and he tells the steps of planting a tree in order. However, Paco put in a sentence that doesn't belong. The paragraph is about planting a tree. We don't need to know about Paco's dancing lessons. Paco's writing would be just fine without that sentence. Draw a line through that sentence. Then, read the paragraph again.

Here is what Mr. Orez wrote about planting the tree. Read his paragraph. Find and draw a line through the sentence that does not belong.

> The park is coming along well. The neighborhood kids had such a good time planting that oak tree last week. It took three of us to get that tree moved into the hole. Next week, I hope to have some flowers to plant. The kids looked pretty funny stomping that dirt down, but they were having fun. That is the whole point of this park.

Lesson 6 Stay on Topic

Paco's sister, Julia, wrote about the new park, too. Read her paragraph. Look for a sentence that is not on topic. When you find it, draw a line through it.

Planting the tree last week was fun, but I can't wait for next week. Mr. Orez said he wants to plant some flowers. I hope the flowers have bright colors. I have a dress with lots of bright colors. They will look so pretty beside the playground.

Can you stay on topic? Write a paragraph about a tree, a park, or a playground. Make sure every sentence belongs.

_____

_____

_____

_____

_____

_____

_____

_____

_____

_____

Chapter 2
Lesson 1 The Writing Process

Good writing starts with a plan. The best writers use the steps in the writing process to plan their writing. Following these five steps leads to good writing.

Step 1: Prewrite
Think of this step as the time to plan. Writers might choose a topic at this point. Or, they might list everything they know about a chosen topic. They might also write down what they need to learn about a topic. Writers might make lists that contain sentences, words, pictures, or charts to begin to put their ideas in order.

Step 2: Draft
Writers put their ideas on paper. This first draft contains sentences and paragraphs. Checking the prewriting notes will help keep the main ideas in order. There will be mistakes in this first draft, and that's okay.

Step 3: Revise
Writers change or fix their first draft. They might decide to move ideas around, put them in a different order, or to add information. They make sure they used clear words that really show readers what they mean. Writers might also take out words or sentences that do not belong.

Step 4: Proofread
Next, writers look over their work again to make sure everything is correct. They look especially for capital letters, end marks, and words that are not spelled correctly.

Step 5: Publish
Finally, writers write a final copy that has no mistakes. They are now ready to share their writing. They might choose to read their work out loud or to create a book. There are many ways for writers to publish their work.

Lesson 1 The Writing Process

What does the writing process look like? Melanie used the writing process to write a paragraph about her grandmother. The steps below are out of order. Label each step with a number and the name of the step.

Step _____ : _____

Saturday afternoons are my favorite time. I go too my grandma's house then. We bake cookies. Usually, we bake our favorites. each week, we write a recipe on a card and put it in a box. Grandma is saving the recipes just for me.

Step _____ : _____

Saturday afternoons are my favorite time. I go too my grandma's house then. We bake cookies. Usually, we bake our favorites. each week, we write a special recipe on a card and put it in a box. Grandma is saving the recipes just for me.

Step _____ : _____

cookies

special recipes

Saturday afternoons

Step _____ : _____

Saturday afternoons are my favorite time. I go to my grandma's house then. We bake cookies. Usually, we bake our favorites. Each week, we write a special recipe on a card and put it in a box. Grandma is saving the recipes just for me.

Step _____ : _____

Saturday afternoons are my favorite time. I go too my grandma's house then. We bake cookies. Usually, we bake our favorites. each week, we write a special recipe on a card and put it in a box. Grandma is saving the recipes just for me.

Lesson 2 List It

Making a list is one way to gather and record ideas before you begin to write. Trey is going to write about his favorite fruit. Here is his list.

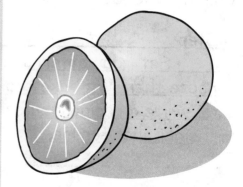

grapefruit: _____
sour _____
sweet _____
sprinkled with sugar _____
pink _____
broiled _____
juicy _____

Mya wants to write about toads. She knows a few things, but she also needs to learn a few things. She listed what she knows. Then, she wrote some questions.

toads: _____
brown _____
lumpy _____
warts? _____
What do they eat? _____
Where do they live? _____

Pretend that you are going to write about a food that you like to eat. List everything you know about the food. Remember to think about how it looks, sounds, smells, feels, and tastes.

_____   _____

_____   _____

_____   _____

_____   _____

Lesson 2 List It

Sometimes, writers use lists to help them choose a topic.

Imagine that your teacher has asked you to write about a memory from your childhood. You have so many memories, you can't decide which one to write about! Start by making a list of different memories you have.

_____   _____

_____   _____

_____   _____

_____   _____

Now, look at the list you just made. Think about each item. Is there one that is especially funny, or one that is especially important to you? Choose one and list details about it. Again, remember to think about how things looked, sounded, smelled, felt, or tasted.

Childhood memory: _____

_____   _____

_____   _____

_____   _____

_____   _____

_____   _____

_____   _____

Lesson 3 Sort Your List

Making a list can really help a writer collect ideas. Sometimes, making a list isn't enough, though. Sometimes, it is helpful to organize the items on a list so they make more sense. Look at Trey's list about grapefruit again. Some of Trey's words tell how the fruit looks and tastes. Some of Trey's words tell how he likes to eat it.

grapefruit: _____
sour _____
sweet _____
sprinkled with sugar _____
pink _____
broiled _____
juicy _____

grapefruit: _____
How it looks and tastes   How I eat it
sour   sprinkled with sugar
sweet   broiled
pink
juicy

Trey rewrote his list. He moved some items around and added some labels.

Now, look at Mya's list. She is still getting ready to write about toads. Could Mya's list be more helpful? Show how you would move items or add labels to make Mya's ideas more organized.

toads: _____   _____
brown _____   _____
lumpy _____   _____
warts? _____   _____
What do they eat? _____   _____
Where do they live? ____   _____

Lesson 3 Sort Your List

Look back at the list you made about a food on page 20. What kinds of words are on your list? Sort the items on your list so that the list is more organized. You might want to add labels, like Trey did, or just write the items in a different order.

_____   _____

_____   _____

_____   _____

_____   _____

Imagine that you must write about an animal for science class. Choose an animal. Then, list all of your ideas about that animal in the first column. After you make your list, look at it closely and see how you might sort the information. Write your organized list in the second column.

<u>List of ideas</u>   <u>My sorted list</u>

_____   _____

_____   _____

_____   _____

_____   _____

_____   _____

_____   _____

NAME _____

Lesson 4 Make an Idea Web

An idea web, or a cluster map, is another good way to collect and organize ideas before you start writing. Marco is going to write about his eighth birthday, which was a special day for him. He wrote his ideas and memories in an idea web.

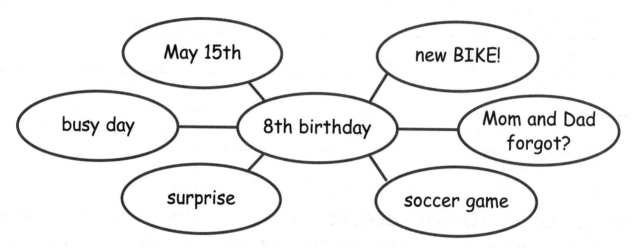

When Marco finished, he looked at his idea web. Some more ideas came to him, so he added them to his web. Notice that his new ideas are not connected to the oval in the center. They are connected to other ideas because they describe or explain the words in those ovals.

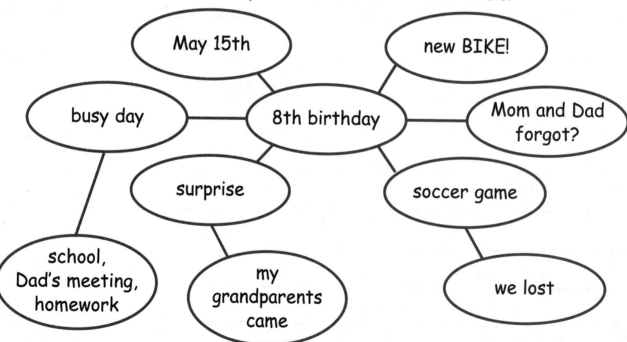

Spectrum Writing
Grade 3
24

Chapter 2 Lesson 4
Organizing Ideas

Lesson 4 Make an Idea Web

What special or important day do you remember? Maybe it was a birthday, the last day of school, or some other day. Choose a special day and create an idea web. If you need to, look back at Marco's web to see how he connected his ideas.

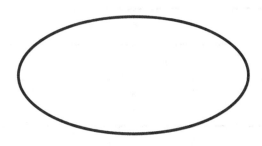

Lesson 5 Make a Time-Order Chart

When writers tell stories, they usually put the events in order. Before they write, writers might use a time-order, or sequence, chart to put their ideas in order.

Kay is writing a story. She made a time-order chart to keep the events in order. Here is part of Kay's chart.

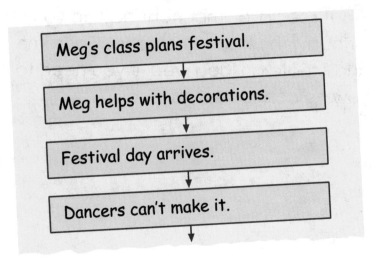

Meg's class plans festival.

Meg helps with decorations.

Festival day arrives.

Dancers can't make it.

Think of a story about a festival or celebration. What interesting event might happen? Think of what events might lead up to the most interesting or exciting part. Record the events in order in the chart below.

Lesson 5 Make a Time-Order Chart

Here is another time-order chart that uses boxes and arrows to show the order of events.

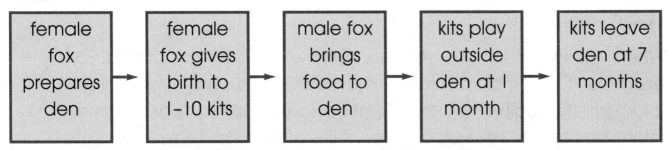

Think of a series of events that you know about. The events might be part of an animal's life cycle, like the fox example above. Or, they might be about an event that you saw or participated in. Think about in what order the events happen. Complete the time-order chart, using as many boxes as you need.

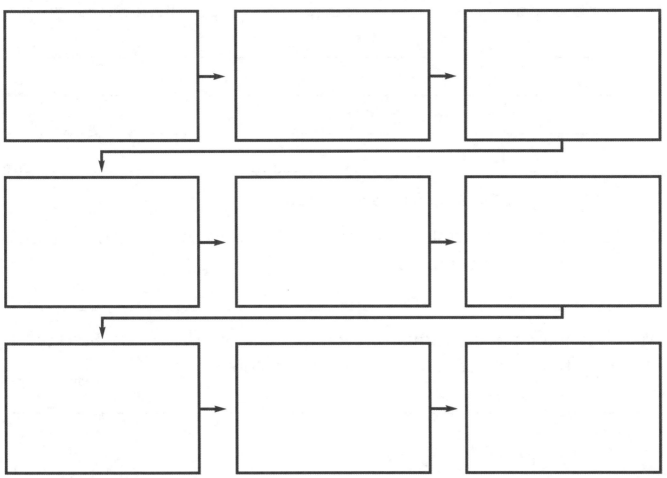

Lesson 6 When Did It Happen?

Remember those fairy tales that begin with "Once upon a time"? "Once upon a time" is not a specific time, but it does give some information about when the story takes place.

When writing, it helps your readers to know when things happen. For example, if your main character is just waking up, what time is it? If it is midnight, the main character might be scared. If it is breakfast time, it might be time to wake up anyway. If it is after noon, maybe your character slept through the whole day!

When could things happen in a story? Think of all the time words or phrases you can. Some ideas are listed below.

| midnight | in the afternoon | April |
| at breakfast | today | three days ago |

_____   _____   _____

_____   _____   _____

_____   _____   _____

_____   _____   _____

Now, use some of the time words you listed.

Write a sentence from a story you might write. Use a time word or phrase at the beginning of your sentence.

_____

Write a sentence about something you did recently. Use a time word or phrase in the middle or at the end of your sentence.

_____

NAME _____

Lesson 6 When Did It Happen?

In addition to time words, transition words help our readers know when things happen and in what order. Here are some common transition words.

after	as soon as	before	during
finally	first	later	meanwhile
next	soon	then	when

Here is an example of some transition words in action. Circle the transition words when you find them. Underline the time words.

> Practice had been over for half an hour, and Mom still hadn't picked me up. I grumbled to myself. Then, as soon as she drove up, I figured it out. This was the day of her big meeting. She was all dressed up. That's why she had been late. Later, I said I was sorry for being mad at her.

Use some transition words in sentences. Use some time words from the list on page 28, as well.

Write about something that happens in the morning.

_____

_____

Write about two things that happen at the same time.

_____

_____

Write about three things that happen in order.

_____

_____

Lesson 7 Use Spatial Order

When writers tell about events, they use time order. When writers describe objects or places, they might use spatial order. In other words, they describe the order of where things are located in space. They might use a left-to-right or top-to-bottom order so that readers can get a clear picture of the object or place.

What is on the left in this picture? What is in the middle? What is on the right? Just as with time order, spatial order has a set of words that help us understand locations. Here are some common spatial words.

above	across	beside	between	beyond
into	left	middle	next to	over
right	through	under		

Look at your teacher's desk. Choose two objects. Where are they? Are they next to each other? Is one on top of the other? Are they close or far away? Write a sentence about the two objects. In the sentence, tell where they are.

_____

_____

Now, look around the room. Describe the general layout to someone who has never seen the room. Imagine that the person is standing in the doorway. Start by describing what he or she will see on the left, then straight ahead, then to the right.

_____

_____

_____

Lesson 7 Use Spatial Order

Would it make sense to describe a classroom from top to bottom?

First, there is the ceiling. Then, there is the wall with the chalkboard. Finally, there is the floor.

That is kind of confusing. However, if you are in a big city, however, a top-to-bottom description might make sense as you look at tall buildings. A bottom-to-top description would work, too. Think of a building or structure you have seen. It might be a house, a statue, or a skyscraper. Close your eyes and try to remember just how it looked. Now, describe it from top to bottom or from bottom to top.

_____

_____

_____

_____

_____

_____

_____

_____

_____

_____

Lesson 7 Use Spatial Order

Steve needs some help. He is writing a story. His character is in a dungeon. It is deep, dark, and creepy. The character is exploring the dungeon to see just how deep, dark, and creepy it really is. Does the character start describing things near the floor and go up? Or, does he look up and work his way down? You decide. Describe the dungeon for Steve.

_____

_____

_____

_____

_____

_____

_____

_____

_____

_____

_____

_____

_____

_____

_____

Lesson 8 How Important Is It?

When writing about an event, time order makes sense. If you are describing a place, spatial order makes sense. There is another method of organization that is useful if you are giving information or if you are writing to persuade. You can organize information by order of importance.

First, think about how a newspaper article gives information. Newspaper reporters know that their readers might not read the entire article, so they state the most important information first. In a newspaper article, the most important information has to do with who is involved, what it is, and where and when it is. Here is an example about a band meeting.

Band Meeting
The Drager Band Boosters will meet at 7 p.m. on Wednesday, August 1. All parents of band members are invited to attend. The fall schedule and new uniforms will be the main topics of discussion.

Write an article for one of these headlines. Make up details for the news story. Remember to give the most important information first. Tell who is involved, what the issue or event is, and where and when it takes place.

New Soccer Practice Schedule   **New Rollercoaster Opens**
Baby Panda Born at Zoo   **Cougars Beat Warriors**

_____

_____

_____

_____

_____

_____

_____

Lesson 8 How Important Is It?

When writing to persuade, the purpose is to make readers think or act in a certain way: for example, persuade classmates to vote for Jane Smith for class president; or, persuade the principal that an after-school nature club is a good idea.

When writing to persuade, save the most important ideas—the strongest arguments—for last. Build ideas from least important to the most important. Here is an example.

> I think Jane Smith should be our class president. There are several good reasons to vote for her. First, she really wants the job. That means she will probably work hard. Second, she has good ideas that will make our classroom a better place. And, finally, she is a good friend to everyone and will work to build a strong classroom community.

Do you have an idea for an after-school club or group? Write a letter to your teacher or principal about the idea. Try to persuade the person that the club is a good idea. Save your strongest, or most important, reason for last.

_____

_____

_____

_____

_____

_____

_____

Lesson 9 Compare It With a Venn

To compare two items, a Venn diagram is a useful tool. Kevin can't decide whether to play soccer or football. He made a Venn diagram to compare the two sports. He wrote things that are the same about the two sports in the center. Things that are different about soccer are in the left circle, and things that are different about football are in the right circle.

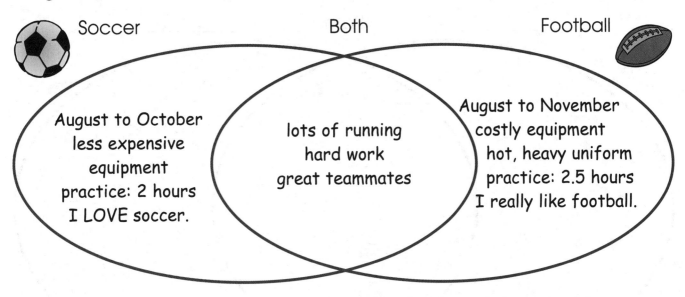

Soccer   Both   Football

August to October
less expensive
equipment
practice: 2 hours
I LOVE soccer.

lots of running
hard work
great teammates

August to November
costly equipment
hot, heavy uniform
practice: 2.5 hours
I really like football.

Now, compare bananas and lemons. Write what is different about bananas in the left circle. Write what is different about lemons in the right circle. Write what is the same about both fruits in the center.

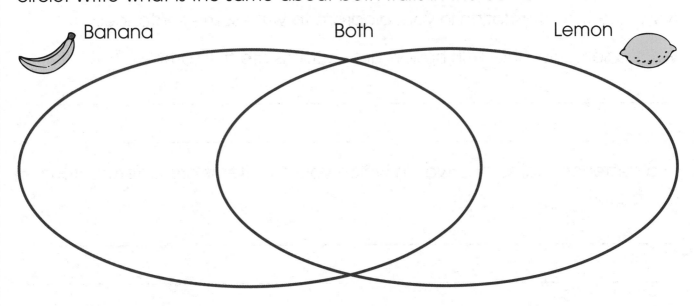

Banana   Both   Lemon

Lesson 9 Compare It With a Venn

What else would you like to compare? Maybe you want to compare third grade with second grade. Or, you could compare two books, two foods, or two kinds of shampoo. Choose the items you want to compare and label the circles. Then, write what is the same and different about the items.

_____   Both   _____

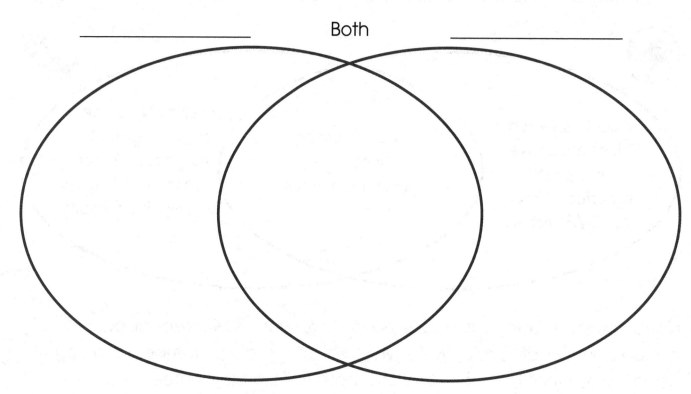

Now, use the information in your diagram to write some sentences.

Write a sentence that tells how your two items are the same.

_____

_____

In a sentence, name one way in which your two items are different from each other.

_____

_____

Lesson 10 How to Compare

When comparing things, tell how they are alike and different. The word ending **–er** and the word *more* help describe how two things are different.

Rock Mountain is <u>taller</u> than Stone Mountain.

Notice how **er** was added to the end of the comparing word *tall*.

Rock Mountain   Stone Mountain

Now compare the mountains using the comparing word *short*. Remember to add the ending. Complete this sentence.

Stone mountain is _____ than Rock Mountain.

Bo is *sadder* than Mo.   Mo is *happier* than Bo.

Notice the change in spelling of the comparing words *sad* and *happy* before adding the **-er** ending. For *sad*, add another **d**, then add **er**. For *happy*, change the **y** to **i**, then add **er**.

Now, try it below.

Sal is _____ Hal.

Hal is _____ Sal.

Sal   Hal

Lesson 10 How to Compare

When using a longer comparing word, do not add **er**. Instead, write the word *more* before the comparing word.

Dan   Stan

Stan's problem is *more dangerous* than Dan's problem.

What could be more comfortable than a bed made of boards? Draw a picture in the box. Then, write a sentence that compares the two beds. Use the word *more* in your sentence.

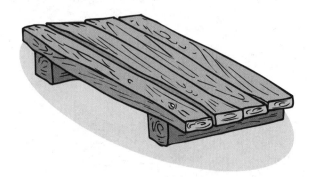

When writing about how three or more things are different, use the ending **-est** or the word *most*.

Ted is the *tallest* player.

What do you know about Tim? Complete the sentence. Use a word that ends in **est**.

Tim is the _____ player.

Tim   Tom   Ted

Lesson 10 How to Compare

Write a complete sentence to answer each question.

Which kite has the longest tail?

_____

_____

Which kite has the shortest tail?

Kite 1   Kite 2   Kite 3

_____

_____

Which kite do you think is the most beautiful?

_____

Compare the trees in this picture.

Write a sentence about one of them. Use *more* or a word with an **-er** ending in your sentence.

_____

_____

Compare the rabbits in this picture. Write a sentence about one of them. Use *most* or a word with an **-est** ending in your sentence.

_____

_____

Chapter 3
Lesson 1 Write for You

Many people write in diaries or journals. One writer might record thoughts and feelings that she does not reveal to other people. Another writer might simply record events and happenings.

Pretend that this is your journal page. Write about yesterday. It might have been a very ordinary day, but that's okay. Remember, when you write in a journal for school, someone will be reading it. When you write in a journal at home, only you will read it.

_____

_____

_____

_____

_____

_____

_____

_____

_____

_____

_____

_____

Lesson 1 Write for You

Another way to record your thoughts and ideas is to keep a learning log. You might jot down a note about something you want to learn more about.

Lewis and Clark—What kinds of animals did they write about in their journals?

You might also record something you learn and want to remember. What have you learned this week? Write down something that you have learned this week.

_____

_____

_____

_____

In a reading log, you could keep track of everything you read. It becomes a handy list to remind you about books you've read, books you especially liked, and maybe even books you didn't care for.

What have you been reading lately? Record their titles and authors below. Rate each book, using words such as *excellent* or *okay*.

_____

_____

_____

_____

Lesson 2 Who Will Read It?

Dr. Platt is a scientist. He knows everything there is to know about platypuses. He is writing to a fellow scientist.

> My study of *Ornithorhynchus anatinu*s has taken a new turn. I am concentrating on the electroreceptors in their snouts. The species' ability to detect prey in this way is probably key to their survival.

Dr. Platt is also writing to his favorite niece. She likes platypuses, too, but she is only 8 years old. He tells her what he is learning about platypuses, but he uses different words than when he wrote to his scientist friend.

A platypus's snout is very special. It has special nerves, or sensors, that can sense the muscle movements of its prey. So, a platypus doesn't even have to see what it's going to eat for lunch! It can sense a frog or an earthworm, even in the mud.

Dr. Platt wrote each letter to a different reader, or audience. He used certain words for one audience, and a different set of words for the other audience.

It is important for all writers to keep their audiences in mind. Writers must think about what the audience knows and what they don't know. They must also think about what the audience is or is not interested in.

Think of something you know a lot about.

What I know about: _____

What I know about it: _____

_____

_____

_____

Lesson 2 Who Will Read It?

Write a paragraph to someone who also knows quite a bit about your specialty. Share a new idea about the topic, or tell about something that happened. Remember, your audience also knows about the topic.

_____

_____

_____

_____

_____

_____

Now, write to someone who does not know much about this special interest of yours. It might be a grandparent, a younger cousin, or a family friend. What might you need to explain? What kinds of words might you need to use? Give the same information, or nearly the same information, as you did in the paragraph at the top of the page. Remember your audience.

_____

_____

_____

_____

_____

_____

Lesson 3 Parts of a Friendly Letter

A friendly letter is a letter written to a family member or friend. It could share family news, personal information, or some good news. Here is a friendly letter that Jennifer wrote to her grandmother.

There is always a comma after the person's name.

There is a **date** at the top.

This is the **greeting**. The word *Dear* always begins with a capital letter.

This is the **body** of the letter.

June 29

Dear Grandma,

Dad just told me your news. I am so sad to hear that Fluffy is sick. You must be sad, too.

I remember when Fluffy was a kitten. She used to chase my feet!

Once, I was sitting at the dinner table. Fluffy jumped up on my lap under the table. She missed my lap, but got my napkin. I got the giggles when I saw her dragging that napkin out of the room.

I hope Fluffy is feeling better by the time you get this letter.

Love,
Jennifer

This is the **closing**. The word may be different, but there is always a comma after the word.

The writer always signs his or her name.

Why do you think Jennifer wrote this letter? _____

_____

_____

Lesson 3 Parts of a Friendly Letter

Grandma wrote back to Jennifer. Copy the parts of Grandma's letter into the right spots on the stationery.

| Dear Jennifer, | July 6 | Love,
Grandma |

Thank you for your letter, dear. Fluffy is much better, now.
I remember seeing Fluffy with that napkin. I went to the kitchen right after that. I had the giggles, too!

Lesson 4 Dear Friend

It is fun to write letters. It is also fun to get letters. If you send a letter to someone, maybe you will get one back! Write the name of each part of this friendly letter.

_____

June 29

_____ → Dear Grandma,

     Dad just told me your news. I am so sad to hear that Fluffy is sick. You must be sad, too.

     I remember when Fluffy was a kitten. She used to chase my feet!

_____ →   Once, I was sitting at the dinner table. Fluffy jumped up on my lap under the table. She missed my lap, but got my napkin. I got the giggles when I saw her dragging that napkin out of the room.

     I hope Fluffy is feeling better by the time you get this letter.

_____ → Love,
     Jennifer

Plan a letter to a friend or classmate. Think about what the person is interested in. What does he or she know about? Write some notes here to help plan what you might write about.

_____   _____

_____   _____

_____   _____

_____   _____

_____   _____

Now, write your letter on the next page. Remember to include all four parts of a friendly letter. Use your neatest printing or handwriting.

Lesson 4 Dear Friend

Lesson 5 Dear Teacher

Writing to a teacher is different from writing to someone who is your own age. You would not begin with "Dear Bart." You would begin with "Dear Mr. Maltin." What else might you need to think about?

Remember that your teacher is older than you are. He or she probably knows some things you don't know. At the same time, your teacher does not know everything about you, so maybe you can teach your teacher something.

Look again at the letter you wrote on page 47. Would that same letter be interesting to your teacher? Answer these questions as you begin to plan a letter to your teacher.

What general topic did you write about in the letter on page 47?

_____

Would your teacher be interested in that topic? Why or why not?

_____

_____

How could you change the topic for your teacher? Think about things you might leave out or things you might explain more fully.

_____

_____

What closing did you use in the letter on page 47? _____

Would you use a different closing for your teacher? If so, what closing?

_____

Write a letter to your teacher on the next page. Include all four parts of a friendly letter.

Lesson 5 Dear Teacher

Lesson 6 It Happened to Me

A **personal narrative** is a true story an author writes about his or her own experiences. Mick wrote a personal narrative about something that happened one day on the way to school.

> ### On the Way to School
>
> Every day was the same. I walked to school past buildings full of windows. I never knew what was behind the windows. Then, something changed.
>
> One day, I was counting sidewalk cracks, as usual, when I heard an amazing sound. Actually, it was lots of sounds. Someone was playing a harp. I looked around until I found the open window.
>
> I forgot all about school. I just stood and stared. I could see a lady with silver hair just inside the window. It looked as if she was hugging the harp. One arm on each side stroked the strings. Low notes and high notes came out all at once. I stood there until she turned and smiled at me. I felt pretty dumb for getting caught staring at her, but I smiled back. Then, she went back to playing. She didn't seem to mind that I was listening.
>
> Now, when I walk to school, I stop at crack number 144. I look up at the harp lady's window. If she is there, I listen for a while. We wave at each other. It's nice to have a friend to wave to on the way to school.

Here are the features of a personal narrative:

- It tells a story about something that happens in a writer's life.
- It is written in the first person, using words such as *I, me,* and *my*.
- It uses time and time-order words to tell events in a sequence.
- It expresses the writer's personal feelings.

Lesson 6 It Happened to Me

Why do people write personal narratives?

They might want to share their thoughts and feelings about something that happened to them. They might also want to entertain their readers. Often, people write to share their feelings and to entertain.

Who reads personal narratives?

If you write a personal narrative, teachers, parents, and classmates might read it. Ask yourself what you want your readers to get from your writing. What might they learn about you?

What can personal narratives be about?

They can be about anything that actually happens to the author. It might be a happy or sad event, a funny situation or a scary one.

What could you write a personal narrative about? Here are some idea starters.

my best day	my worst moment	my first swimming lesson
my greatest accomplishment		my biggest mistake
My picture was in the newspaper because....		
how I met my best friend		I never worked so hard as when....
I was so embarrassed when....		I was so mad when....

Now, choose a few ideas that you like. Jot some notes about each one. One of these might be the start of a great personal narrative.

Starter: _____

_____

Starter: _____

_____

Starter: _____

_____

Lesson 7 The Writing Process: Personal Narrative

Writing a personal narrative gives you a chance to share an important or funny event with your readers. As you write, you may even discover something about yourself. First, review the steps of the writing process.

Prewrite: Choose a topic. Collect ideas. Make lists or charts. Organize ideas.

Draft: Write ideas down on paper in sentences.

Revise: Fix mistakes in draft. Add details. Change things around to make the writing better. Rewrite the sentences.

Proofread: Check for final mistakes in spelling, capitalization, and punctuation.

Publish: Make a final, error-free copy. Share with readers.

Prewrite

Personal narratives do not have to be about amazing races, life-and-death rescues, or unbelievable events. They can be about very ordinary things. Remember the narrative you read on page 50? Mick wrote about walking to school.

Look again at the ideas on page 51 and the notes you made. Choose one of those ideas, or another idea that you like, and begin to explore it here.

My idea: _____

List as many details as you can think of quickly. Remember the event and its sights, sounds, smells, and tastes.

_____   _____

_____   _____

_____   _____

Lesson 7 The Writing Process: Personal Narrative

Choosing a topic is an important step. If your topic is too big, you'll be writing forever. If your topic is too small, you won't have enough to say. Here are some examples.

Shawna wanted to write about second grade, her favorite year so far. Well, a lot happened in second grade. That's too much to cover. So, Shawna tried to think about just one part of second grade. She wrote about her teacher, Mrs. Carlson.

Steve wanted to write about what he got for his birthday. He listed his presents. Well, there's more to a birthday than just presents. Steve's readers might be more interested in how Steve's family celebrates. Steve wrote about his birthday celebration and his presents.

Think about the idea you started to explore on page 52. Ask yourself these questions.

- Can I think of plenty of details to make my writing interesting?

- Do I think I can cover my idea in about one page?

- Will my topic be interesting to my readers?

If you don't think your topic will work, go back to page 52 and develop another one. If you do think your topic will work, begin organizing your ideas. Use the idea web below. Write your topic in the center. Add circles, as needed, to connect your ideas and details.

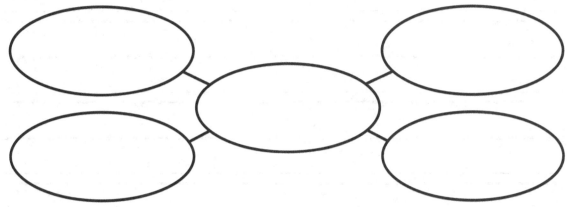

Lesson 7 The Writing Process: Personal Narrative

Now it is time to put your ideas in order. Think about the story you are about to tell in your personal narrative. Use the sequence chart on this page to list the events, in order.

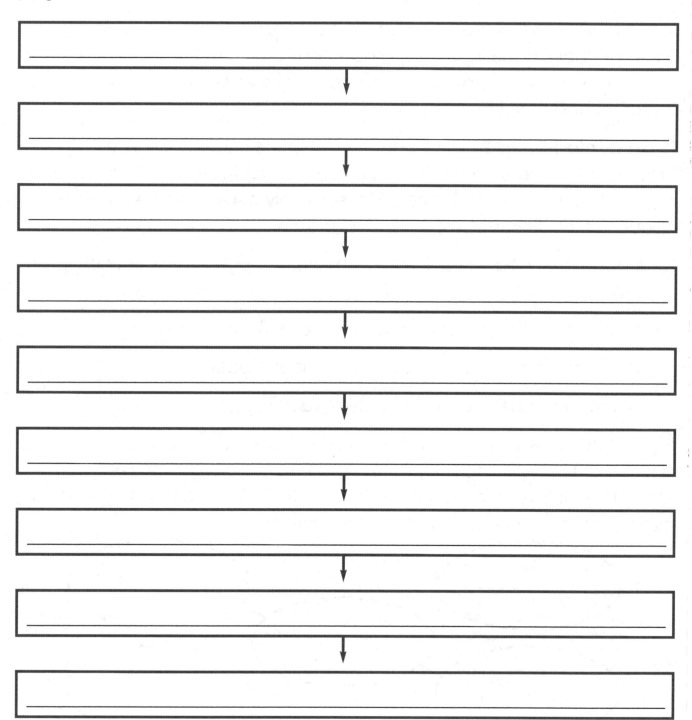

Lesson 7 The Writing Process: Personal Narrative

Draft

It is time to write a first draft of your personal narrative. Look back at your sequence chart whenever you need to. Write your personal narrative on this page. As you write, don't worry about misspelled words. Just get your ideas down in sentences and in order.

_____

_____

_____

_____

_____

_____

_____

_____

_____

_____

_____

_____

_____

Write an idea for a title. It is okay if it changes later.

Title: _____

Lesson 7 The Writing Process: Personal Narrative

Revise

One of the hardest things for any writer to do is to fix, or change, his or her own work. Writers put thought and effort into their work. It's hard not to read even a first draft and think that it is perfect. However, good writers know that they can almost always improve their first drafts.

Answer these questions about your draft. If you answer "no" to any of these questions, then those are the areas that might need improvement. Feel free to make marks on your draft, so you know what needs more work.

- Did you tell about just one event or one "thing" in your narrative?

- Did you include details to make readers feel as if they are right there with you?

- Did you tell events in order? Did you use time-order words to show when events happened?

- Did you tell how you felt about the events? Do readers get a sense of your personal feelings?

- Did you use verbs and nouns that really say what you mean?

- How does your story sound when you read it aloud? Does it have both short and long sentences to make it interesting?

Look back through your draft and underline the action words. Did you use the same ones over and over? Did you use words that show the action? Here's an example.

rang out   crept
The sound ~~happened~~ again. Dad and I looked at each other. We ~~went~~ down the stairs. We didn't see anything unusual.

Lesson 7 The Writing Process: Personal Narrative

Write the revision of your first draft below. As you revise, remember to make sure your action words are really active.

_____

_____

_____

_____

_____

_____

_____

_____

_____

_____

_____

_____

_____

_____

Are you still happy with your title? If not, now is your chance to change it.

Title: _____

Lesson 7 The Writing Process: Personal Narrative

Proofread

Now is the time to correct those last little mistakes. Proofreading is easier if you look for just one kind of error at a time. So, read through once for capital letters. Read your narrative again for end punctuation. Then, read again for spelling. Here is a checklist to help you as you proofread your revised narrative.

_____ Each sentence begins with a capital letter.
_____ Each sentence ends with the correct punctuation (period, question mark, or exclamation point).
_____ Each sentence states a complete thought.
_____ All words are spelled correctly. (If you're not sure, check a dictionary.)

When proofreaders work, they use certain symbols. Using these symbols makes proofreading easier

- three little lines under a letter mean that something should be capitalized. Write the capitalized letter above it.

- If there is a period missing, do this⊙

- Can you insert a question mark like this?

- Don't forget your exclamation points!

- Fix misspelled words like tis.

Use these symbols as you proofread your personal narrative. Remember to read your writing out loud. Sometimes it is easier to catch mistakes when reading out loud.

Lesson 7 The Writing Process: Personal Narrative

Publish

Write a final copy of your personal narrative. Write carefully and neatly so that there are no mistakes.

_____

_____

_____

_____

_____

_____

_____

_____

_____

_____

_____

_____

_____

_____

_____

_____

_____

_____

_____

Chapter 4
Lesson 1 Use Complete Sentences

NAME _____

You already know that a sentence is a group of words that states a complete thought. You also know that a sentence begins with a capital letter and ends with a period, a question mark, or an exclamation point. Here are some complete and correct sentences.

> Dogs howled.
> The wind blew all night.
> After the storm, we went out on the porch and looked at the fallen tree, which lay across the yard, covering the swing set, the garden shed, and the car in the driveway.

As you can see, complete sentences can be very short, very long, or in between. Here's a closer look at what makes a complete sentence.

Wind is the **subject**. It is the person or thing that **does the action**. *The wind* is the complete subject.	The wind (blew all night.)	*Blew* is the **predicate**. It is the **action**. *Blew all night* is the complete predicate.

If a sentence is missing either a subject or a predicate, it is not complete. It is called a **fragment**. Here are some sentence fragments.

> Walked through the puddles. (This fragment has no subject.)
> The water up to my ankles. (This fragment has no action word.)

Write whether each item is a sentence or a fragment. If it is a sentence, underline the complete subject and circle the complete predicate. Write *missing a subject* or *missing a predicate* next to each fragment.

The storm came suddenly. _____

Blew down many trees. _____

The wind so strong and steady. _____

Lesson 1 Use Complete Sentences

Sometimes, there is too much information in one sentence. When that happens, it might be a **run-on sentence**. A run-on sentence is actually two sentences that are joined without any punctuation. Here is an example.

The wind picked up I could hear it even in the basement.

To correct this, make two sentences out of the run-on sentence, like this:

The wind picked up. I could hear it even in the basement.

Or, join the two sentences with a comma and *or, but,* or *and.* In this case, *and* works best.

The wind picked up, and I could hear it even in the basement.

Remember, a run-on sentence is two or more complete sentences that are joined without any punctuation.

Write whether each item is a complete sentence or a run-on sentence.

_____ I heard a crash it was up in the kitchen.

_____ Mom went upstairs I stayed in the basement.

_____ She looked around because she was sure a window had broken.

_____ It was the cat he had knocked over a plant.

Look back at the items you marked as run-on sentences. Can you correct them? Use proofreading symbols from page 58 to show how you would correct the run-on sentences.

Lesson 2 Action!

Usually, the subject of a sentence does the action. That is easy to see in this sentence:

> Zack blew a whistle.

The verb in the sentence is an **active verb** because the subject does the action.

What about this sentence?

> A whistle was blown.

First, make sure it is a complete sentence. It has a subject and a predicate, so it is a sentence. *Whistle* is the subject of the sentence. However, the whistle does not do the action, the whistle "receives" the action. The verb, *was blown*, is a **passive verb**, because the subject does not do the action.

Passive verbs are always two-part verbs. They always have one of these helping verbs—*am, is, was, be, been*—plus a main verb. However, just because you see one of those helping verbs, it does not mean the verb is passive.

> Passive verb: Anne **was** *pulled* in the wagon.

> Active verb: Anne **was** *happy* to be riding.

How can you tell the difference? Ask yourself these two questions: What is the subject? Is the subject doing the action?

If the answer to the second question is "yes," then you have an active verb. If the answer is "no," you have a passive verb.

Sometimes, it is not known who did the action, so a passive verb must be used, such as, "The window was broken." Most of the time, however, writing will be more clear and easier to read with active verbs.

Lesson 2 | Action!

Compare these two paragraphs. The one on the left is written mostly with passive verbs. The one on the right is written mostly with active verbs. What do you notice?

The parade was started right at 3 p.m. when a whistle was blown by Zack. The parade was led by Mr. Stoltzman. The first-graders were led in by Mrs. Kraft. Anne Connor, who has a broken leg, was pulled in a wagon by Amy Wheeler. The second-graders were allowed to ride their bikes by Mr. Garcia. The parade was enjoyed by everyone.	The parade started right at 3 p.m. when Zack blew a whistle. Mr. Stoltzman led the parade. Mrs. Kraft led the first-graders. Amy Wheeler pulled Anne Connor, who has a broken leg, in a wagon. Mr. Garcia allowed the second-graders to ride their bikes. Everyone enjoyed the parade.

Underline the subject of each sentence. Put an **X** next to each sentence that contains a passive verb.

_____ Tyler was watching the parade.

_____ Popcorn was eaten by everyone.

_____ Mrs. Kraft was surprised by the whistle.

_____ The mess was cleaned up after the parade.

Lesson 3 How To Do It

A process is a series of actions that lead toward a goal or product. You do processes every day. Getting up and going to school is a process. Eating your lunch is a process. Even picking teams for a game at recess is a process.

Mr. O'Malley says, "Homework is a process." Here are the three steps that Mr. O'Malley listed on the board:

1. Take the homework home.
2. Do the homework.
3. Return the completed homework to school.

The steps Mr. O'Malley listed tell about a simple process. Other processes have more steps and require a little more thought. They might also require instructions. When you follow instructions, you know that you must do them in order. When you write instructions, you must also do them in order, just like Mr. O'Malley did.

The first step in telling how to do a process is to list the steps in order. Think of something simple, such as making your bed or feeding a pet. What steps are there? In what order should they be done? Write them below.

How to _____

1. _____

2. _____

3. _____

4. _____

5. _____

Lesson 3 How To Do It

Remember your audience when writing. Who might read your instructions? Do they know a lot about the topic? Or, might some of the words or ideas be new to them? How much explaining must you do?

Imagine that you must tell a 5-year-old how to do something, such as play a simple game or put together a simple snack. List the steps here. Keep them clear and simple.

How to _____

1. _____

2. _____

3. _____

4. _____

5. _____

Read your two sets of instructions above and on Page 64 again. Is everything very clear? Did you use action words and describing words that say exactly what you mean? For example, if you told how to make a bed, did you say, "Pull the sheet up"? Would it be better to say, "Pull the sheet up tight"?

Find places where you might add details or change plain words to more clear words. Choose several steps that you can make better. Rewrite them here.

_____

_____

_____

_____

_____

NAME _____

Lesson 4 Fact or Opinion

People like to share the facts they know whenever they get the chance. Others like to share their opinions, whether anyone asks for them or not. There is a right and a wrong time to use facts and opinions.

> **fact** *noun* something known to be true or real; something real; something that can be proven true
>
> **opinion** *noun* a belief; a personal judgment

When your teacher asks a question in class, he or she is usually looking for an answer that is a fact.

Question: What is the main ingredient in paper?
Answer: wood

That is a fact.

Think about this question.

Question: Is recycling paper a good thing?

This question is looking for an opinion. Here is how some students answered the question. They stated their opinions, and then they used facts to support their opinions.

Answer: Yes. Recycling paper saves trees.
Answer: Yes, because the landfills are filling up with paper.

Read these sentences. Label the opinions with an **O**. Label the facts with an **F**.

_____ Recycling paper is the only sensible thing to do.

_____ Recycled paper is less expensive to produce than new paper.

_____ I prefer recycled paper to new paper.

Spectrum Writing
Grade 3
66

Chapter 4 Lesson 4
Writing to Inform or Explain

Lesson 4 Fact or Opinion

When writing, be careful when it comes to facts and opinions. Make sure you are writing facts. If you are writing opinions, make sure they were asked for. Also, make sure you support your opinions with facts.

Think of a subject about which you have an opinion. It might be recycling, school uniforms, or your favorite music. Write two opinions about the subject.

Opinion 1:_____

_____

Opinion 2:_____

_____

Now, write two facts about the same subject.

Fact 1: _____

_____

Fact 2: _____

_____

Finally, write an opinion and support it with a fact. If you need to, look back at page 66 to see how the students supported their opinions about recycling paper.

_____

_____

_____

_____

_____

Lesson 5 This Is How It Happened

Paul saw a basketball game last night, and it was a great game. His school's team won, and he is eager to write about it for the school newspaper. His first step was to list the important events in order.

    1. At half time, the Bobcats were behind by 12 points.
    2. Teams returned to the floor, and the Bobcats were fired up.
    3. The Bobcats scored 10 points before the Bulldogs even knew what happened.
    4. The teams traded baskets right up to the final seconds.
    5. Jackson made the play of the night, pushing the Bobcats ahead by 2 points to win.

Paul included important details from the game, and he put them in order. He also included some opinions. In item #2, "the Bobcats were fired up" is an opinion. Can you find two other opinions in the list? Circle them.

Paul's opinions make the information about the game more interesting. They help you feel as if you were there, watching the action.

Here is a list of events from the Bulldogs' point of view. Like Paul's list, it gives events in order. Also like Paul, the writer included opinions. When you find them, circle them.

    1. The Bulldogs played very well during the first half.
    2. At half time, they led the game by 12.
    3. The Bulldogs started the second half with a little too much confidence.
    4. The Bobcats went on a scoring streak.
    5. The Bulldogs were unable to stop the Bobcats from making the winning basket.

Lesson 5 This Is How It Happened

Think about what you have done so far today. List some of today's events, in order. If you include any opinions, circle them.

1. _____

2. _____

3. _____

4. _____

5. _____

Now, think of something a little more exciting. Think of an event that you have seen or been to recently. It might be a sporting event, a concert, or a neighborhood party. Write some of the important or interesting things that happened in order. If you include opinions, circle them.

1. _____

_____

2. _____

_____

3. _____

_____

4. _____

_____

5. _____

_____

Lesson 6 Special Instructions

Have you ever looked at the instructions for putting together a bicycle? Did they look pretty tough? That's because those instructions were written for an adult. The writer assumed that an adult would know about certain tools and how to use them.

Write instructions for making a greeting card. Your instructions will be included in a book of project ideas for first-graders. You need to make your instructions simple and clear for your first-grade readers. Remember to put the steps in order. Include drawings in the space on the right if you think they will help your readers understand.

How to Make a Greeting Card
(for first-graders)

_____

_____

_____

_____

_____

_____

_____

_____

_____

_____

Lesson 6 Special Instructions

Your greeting card ideas are so good that you have been asked to write some more instructions. This time, they will be for teenagers. How might you need to change your instructions for your teenage readers? What details might you add to make the project interesting to or challenging for teenagers? Write your new set of instructions here. Include drawings if you think they will be helpful. It is still important to put the steps in order.

How to Make a Greeting Card
(for teenagers)

_____

_____

_____

_____

_____

_____

_____

_____

_____

_____

_____

_____

_____

Lesson 7 It Is Just Around the Corner

You are walking into the lunchroom when a new student walks up and asks you how to get to the nurse's office. Do you know the way? Can you give clear directions to help the other student find the way?

Directions, just like how-to instructions, need to be in order. They also need to tell *where*. Here are some words to help you write clear directions.

Direction Words	Position Words	Time-Order Words
left	over	first
right	under	second
up	past	then
down	beyond	next
north	before	after that
west	above	finally
	beside	

At Jamie's school, this is how to get from the lunchroom to the nurse's office. Notice how Jamie uses some of the words from the lists above. Circle each one that you find.

First, go down this hallway. When you get to the end, turn left. Walk past the main office. Then, the nurse's office is the second door on the right.

Lesson 7 It Is Just Around the Corner

Write directions that tell how to get from your classroom to the lunchroom. If you need to, close your eyes and imagine yourself walking there. Now, write your directions. If you need to, look back on page 72 for direction, position, and time-order words to use.

_____

_____

_____

_____

_____

Imagine you live in a castle on a hill. You have to walk all the way to the next hill to get to school. Between your castle and the school is a town. What streets must you follow? How do you know where to turn? If it helps, draw a sketch that shows the castle,  the town, and the school. Write directions to help someone find the way.

_____

_____

_____

_____

_____

Lesson 8   Ask the Right Question

The first lesson that reporters learn is how to ask questions. And their questions are always based on the words *who, what, when, where, why,* and *how*. You can use these questions, too, to find out many things.

Beth's class is studying families. Beth is supposed to ask a family member some questions. She started planning her questions below. Can you finish Beth's questions for her? Think about the kinds of questions you would ask a family member.

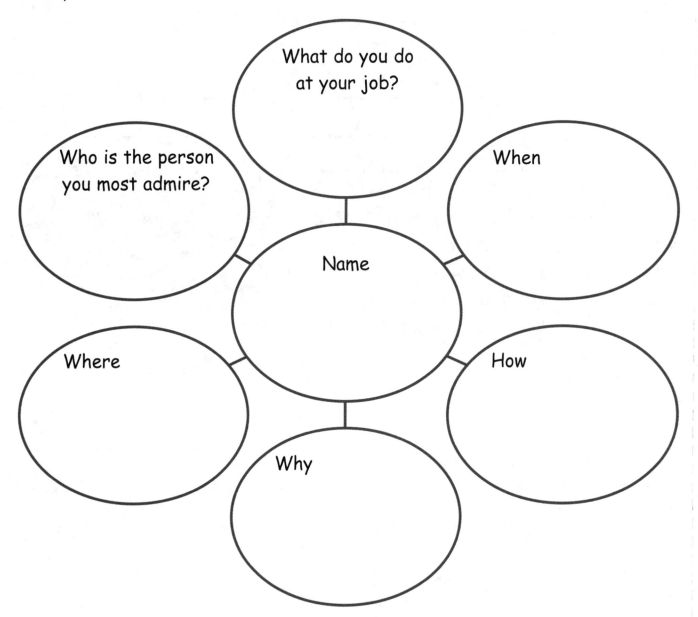

Lesson 8 Ask the Right Question

If you could interview anyone in the world, whom would you choose? Would it be the president or some other world leader? Would it be a doctor, a musician, or an astronaut? Remember, it could be anyone.

Imagine your interview is next week. Now, prepare your questions. What will you ask this special person? You may ask more than one question with each question word. Write your questions below.

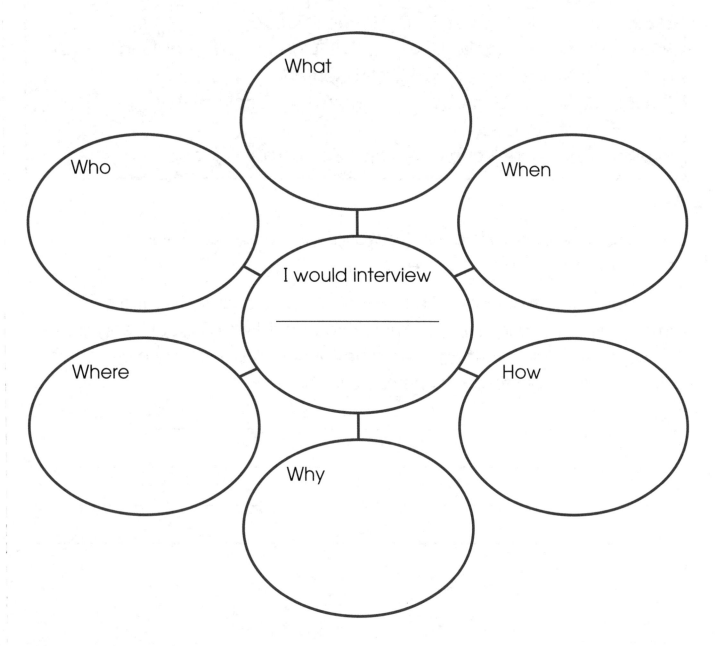

Lesson 9 The Writing Process: News Story

A news story is an account of something that has happened. A news story might be about a natural disaster, such as a storm or an earthquake. Or, it might be about the circus that came to town.

Before you write a news story, review the steps of the writing process.

Prewrite: Choose a topic. Collect ideas. Make lists or charts. Organize ideas.

Draft: Write ideas down on paper in sentences.

Revise: Fix mistakes in draft. Add details. Change things around to make the writing better. Rewrite the sentences.

Proofread: Check for final mistakes in spelling, capitalization, and punctuation.

Publish: Make a final, error-free copy. Share with readers.

Prewrite

Every city, town, and village in the world has news, even if it is important only to the people in that place.

What news story would you like to write? Will you choose to write about a famous person or a person you know? You could write about penguins in Antarctica, the fish in a local river, a new invention, or a very old machine. Write some possible topics for news stories here.

_____   _____

_____   _____

_____   _____

_____   _____

Lesson 9 The Writing Process: News Story

Look over the ideas you recorded on page 76. Which one seems the best? Choose one and write it below.

My idea: _____

What do you know about this topic? What might you need to learn about this topic? Write down pieces of information that you know or need to find out.

_____   _____

_____   _____

_____   _____

_____   _____

Even if you're not interviewing a person, you can still ask yourself questions that begin with *who, what, where, when, why,* and *how.* Asking these questions will provide information to you. Think of questions that you would like to answer in your news story. Write them here.

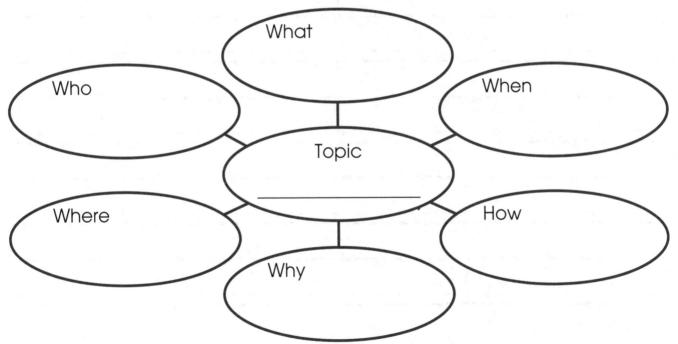

Lesson 9 The Writing Process: News Story

So far, you have been choosing a topic and collecting ideas. Now it is time to put your ideas in order. Think about the news story you are about to write. Use the sequence chart on this page to put your information into an order that makes sense. You might use time order, order of importance, or spatial order. Think about what fits best with your topic.

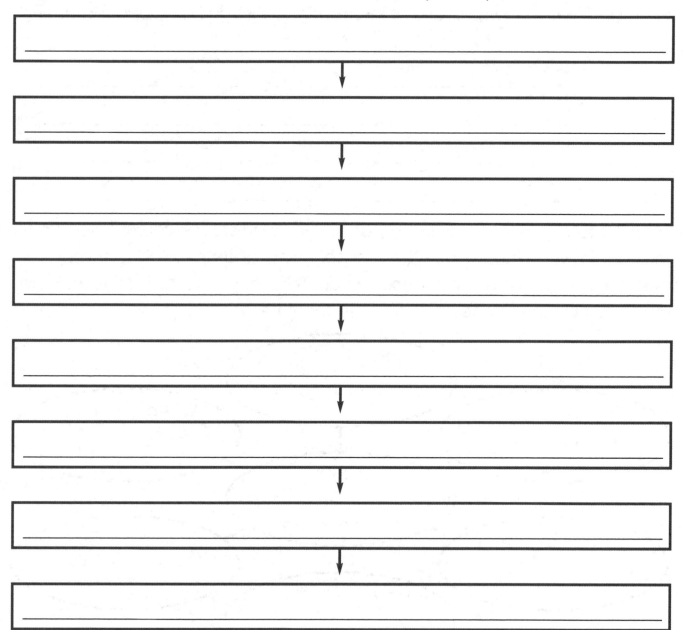

Lesson 9 The Writing Process: News Story

Draft

It is time to write a first draft of your news story. As you write, look at the chart on page 78 to keep your ideas in order. Write your news story on this page. Continue on another sheet of paper if you need to. Do not worry about misspelled words or punctuation for now. Just write your ideas down in sentences and in order.

_____

_____

_____

_____

_____

_____

_____

_____

_____

_____

_____

_____

_____

Write an idea for a headline here. You can change it later.

Headline: _____

Lesson 9 The Writing Process: News Story

Revise

People who write news stories know that they must look over their work carefully. Once it is printed in the newspaper, it is too late to fix a mistake. So, they reread their news stories and think about ways to make them better. Here are some questions to ask about the first draft of your own news story. If you answer "no" to any of these questions, those are the areas that might need improvement. Feel free to make marks on your draft, so you know what needs more work.

- Does your news story answer the questions *Who?*, *What?*, *Where?*, *When?*, *Why?*, and *How?*
- Is the information in your news story clearly presented? Do details fit together in a way that makes sense to readers?
- If you expressed opinions, did you support them with facts?
- Does your news story begin with a sentence that grabs readers' attention and makes them want to keep reading?
- Will readers get the idea that you are interested in this topic? Did you give them a sense of why the topic is interesting?
- Did you use verbs and nouns that really say what you mean?
- Did you read your news story out loud? Did you include sentences of different lengths to make it sound interesting?

First, focus on making sure your information is correct and that it will be clear to your readers. Look back through your draft and underline the facts. Are you sure about all of them? Do you need to check an encyclopedia or the person you interviewed again? Now is the time to make sure everything is correct.

Lesson 9 The Writing Process: News Story

Write the revision of your first draft here. As you revise, keep your audience in mind. Make sure you are presenting information in a clear manner.

_____

_____

_____

_____

_____

_____

_____

_____

_____

_____

_____

_____

_____

Now that you have revised your draft, are you still happy with your headline? If not, write a new one below.

Headline: _____

Lesson 9 The Writing Process: News Story

Proofread

Now, correct the last mistakes. Proofreading is easier if you look for just one kind of error at a time. First, read through it once for capital letters. Read it again for end punctuation. Then, read it again for spelling. Here is a checklist to help you as you proofread your revised news story.

_____ Each sentence begins with a capital letter.
_____ Each sentence ends with the correct punctuation (period, question mark, or exclamation point).
_____ Each sentence states a complete thought.
_____ All words are spelled correctly.

When proofreaders work, they use certain symbols. Using these symbols makes their job easier. They will make your job easier, too.

- three little lines under a letter mean that something should be capitalized. Write the capitalized letter above it.

- If there is a period missing, do this ⊙ •

- Can you insert a question mark like this ?

- Don't forget your exclamation points !

- Fix misspelled words like this tis.

Use these symbols as you proofread your news story. Remember to read your writing out loud, even if there is no one to listen. Sometimes it is easier to catch mistakes when reading out loud.

NAME _____

Lesson 9 The Writing Process: News Story

Publish

On page 83, write a final copy of your news story. When you are finished, share your news story with a friend or classmate.

_____

_____

_____

_____

_____

_____

_____

_____

_____

_____

_____

_____

_____

_____

_____

_____

_____

Chapter 5
Lesson 1 Use Your Senses

If you were standing in this kitchen, just think what would be around you. You would see the steaming plates of food and hear the clattering of pans. You would surely smell a mixture of foods lined up on the smooth countertop. And, if you were lucky, you would get to taste something salty, spicy, or sweet. In other words, you would learn about the kitchen by using all five of your senses: seeing, hearing, smelling, touching, and tasting.

If you were to describe this kitchen to someone else, you should use all five of your senses. How do you use your senses when you write? You use words that help readers use their senses.

Look again at the picture. What do you see? List some things here. Remember to help your reader see things, too. For example, do you see a "large pot," or a "large, red pot"?

What I see: _____ _____

_____ _____ _____

Now, use your other senses and write what you would hear, smell, touch, and taste in this kitchen.

What I hear: _____ _____

What I smell: _____ _____

What I touch: _____ _____

What I taste: _____ _____

Lesson 1 Use Your Senses

Look back at the lists you made on page 84. Did you remember to use good sense words so that readers can see, hear, smell, touch, and taste what is in the kitchen? For example, if you said that you hear voices in this kitchen, ask yourself what kind of voices they might be. Are they happy, angry, quiet, or loud ones? Review your list, and see if you can add any other words that more clearly describe the kitchen.

Now, put your words to work. Describe this kitchen so clearly that your reader will feel as if he or she is actually standing right in the middle of it. For this paragraph, organize your ideas by sense. First, tell what you saw, then what you heard, then what you smelled, touched, and tasted. Remember to indent the first sentence of your paragraph.

_____

_____

_____

_____

_____

_____

_____

_____

_____

_____

_____

Lesson 2 Make a Riddle

You can put your senses to work and make some riddles. Here is a riddle that Tam wrote.

> _____ What is long and skinny, soft on one end and pointed at the other, and gets smaller as you use it?

Do you know what it is? You probably have one on your desk right now. It is a pencil.

For her riddle, Tam used a common object and turned it into a mystery. She told what it looks like, long and skinny, and how it feels, soft and pointed. Then, she added one other detail, gets smaller, to make her riddle interesting.

Write your own riddle. Use a sheet of paper as the answer of the riddle. First, use your senses to learn about the paper. Some details are already filled in for you.

What does a piece of paper

look like? _____

smell like? has no smell _____

sound like? _____

feel like? _____

taste like? (does not apply) _____

Now, use what you know about this piece of paper to write a riddle.

What is _____

_____

Lesson 2 Make a Riddle

Write another riddle, this time using a book as the answer.
Record some details here. Then, write your riddle.

What does a book

look like? _____

smell like? _____

sound like? _____

feel like? _____

taste like? _____

Riddle: _____

_____

Choose another common object, but don't tell anyone what you're
choosing. Record details about the object here. Then, write a riddle and
share it with someone. See how long it takes your reader to guess the
answer.

What does a _____

look like? _____

smell like? _____

sound like? _____

feel like? _____

taste like? _____

Riddle: _____

_____

Lesson 3 This Is A Room

If you walked into this room, you would probably look from one side to the other. Most likely, you would look to the left first, then the center, and then to the right. List some details about the room here.

On the left	In the center	On the right

Organizing details from left to right (or from top to bottom) is called **spatial organization**. It is up to you to give readers all the information they need. Remember to include information about sizes and shapes (a huge oval mirror), colors (a bright pink carpet), and textures (a lumpy sofa).

Study the picture some more and think about what you would see, hear, smell, feel, and taste if you were standing in the room. Now, write a description of the room in the picture. Give details in order from left to center to right.

_____

_____

_____

_____

Lesson 3 This Is A Room

Think of a room in your own home. It might be your bedroom or another room. Close your eyes and imagine it. What is on the left, center, and right? Make some notes about the room here. Remember to use sense words.

Now, write a paragraph in which you describe this room. Again, use spatial organization to present details from left to right to describe what you would see in the room.

_____

_____

_____

_____

_____

_____

_____

_____

_____

_____

Questions to Ask About a Descriptive Paragraph

Does the paragraph give details that clearly describe the place?
Does the paragraph present ideas in an order that makes sense, such as from left to right?
Does the paragraph use sense words so that readers can see, hear, smell, feel, and taste what is being described?
Is the first sentence of the paragraph indented?

NAME _____

Lesson 4 Imagine a Setting

You are writing a great story. Where does the action take place? Is it in a mad scientist's laboratory? In a desert? In a space-age classroom? Where the story happens is part of the setting.

First, write down as many ideas for story settings as you can think of. Even if an idea doesn't seem really interesting, list it here anyway. You might end up combining ideas.

Setting ideas: _____ _____ _____

_____ _____ _____

Now, think about when your great story will take place: in the past, in the present, or in the future. Time is also part of the setting. Imagine each place you listed above in the past, present, and future. Write your favorite idea below.

Place: _____

Time: _____

What is there to see? What sounds and smells are there? What textures and tastes?

Sights: _____

Sounds: _____

Smells: _____

Textures: _____

Tastes: _____

Review the details you have recorded. Can you really imagine the place?

Lesson 4 Imagine a Setting

Now, describe the setting of your story. Remember to organize your details in a way that makes sense. For example, if you are describing a room, you might go from left to right. If you are describing a tall rocket ship, you might go from bottom to top. If you are describing an outdoor setting, you might go from near to far. Think about which method makes most sense for your setting.

_____

_____

_____

_____

_____

_____

_____

_____

_____

_____

_____

_____

On Your Own

Now that your setting is ready, write the story on a separate piece of paper. You may use the description of the setting as is, or you can write details from the description into your story as needed.

Lesson 5 Vary Sentence Structure

Mark wrote a description of his uncle's barn.

In the barn, there are many things to see. In the hayloft, hay bales are piled high. On the wall, there are tools hanging all in a row. In the pen, sheep make soft little sounds. Through the stall windows, the horses beg for sugar.

Mark's paragraph is well organized, but it is not interesting. He started every one of his sentences with the same type of phrase that tells *where*. His description would be more interesting if he used sentences of different lengths and with different word order. Here is a revised version of Mark's paragraph. Notice that the words are almost exactly the same.

There are many things to see in the barn. Hay bales are piled high in the hayloft. Tools hang on the wall. They are all in a row. Sheep make soft little sounds in their pen. The horses beg for sugar through the stall windows.

Write a description of this farm scene. In your paragraph, use a variety of short, medium, and long sentences. Do not begin all of your sentences the same way.

_____

_____

_____

_____

_____

_____

_____

Lesson 5 Vary Sentence Structure

Using short, medium, and long sentences in your writing helps it to be more interesting. Here are some other ways to make your sentences different and more interesting.

Begin with a word or phrase that tells *where*.	Over the barn roof, the sun rose.
Begin with a word or phrase that tells *when*.	In the morning, I like to be in the barn.
Begin with a word that tells *how*.	Slowly, I climbed up the wooden ladder.
Begin with the subject.	The barn is my favorite place to be.
Begin with action.	Pitching hay for the horses is hard work.

Write another description. It may be of the barn scene on page 92, or you may choose to describe something else. Keep in mind all of the ways to make your sentences different.

_____

_____

_____

_____

_____

_____

_____

Lesson 6 The Writing Process: Descriptive Writing

Writers use descriptive writing in many ways. Descriptive writing can play a big part is some stories. It is also important in nonfiction. We are going to use your own experience as the base for a descriptive passage. You will describe observations you have made or events you have seen.

First, review the steps of the writing process.

Prewrite: Choose a topic. Collect ideas. Make lists or charts. Organize ideas.

Draft: Write ideas down on paper in sentences.

Revise: Fix mistakes in draft. Add details. Change things around to make the writing better. Rewrite the sentences.

Proofread: Check for final mistakes in spelling, capitalization, and punctuation.

Publish: Make a final, error-free copy. Share with readers.

Prewrite

Your descriptive writing may take the form of an observation report, such as watching a plant grow and develop. Your descriptive writing may take the form of an eyewitness account, such as watching a storm from the safety of your home. Start by simply listing your first ideas about observations you have made or events you have seen.

_____   _____

_____   _____

_____   _____

_____   _____

Lesson 6 The Writing Process: Descriptive Writing

Choose one idea from page 94 that you think might work. In the space below, freewrite for two minutes, writing down absolutely everything you can think of about the idea.

Did your thoughts flow freely, or did you struggle to find things to write down? If you wrote easily, there's a good chance that the idea will work. If you had a hard time thinking of anything, choose another idea and freewrite about it on a separate sheet of paper. Continue until you find a topic idea about which your ideas flow easily.

Once you decide on a topic, you can collect details. Use this chart to record details. Use information from your freewriting, and write new ideas.

What I Saw	What I Heard	What I Smelled

What I Felt	What I Tasted

Lesson 6 The Writing Process: Descriptive Writing

So far, you have been choosing a topic, collecting ideas, and recording details. Now, it is time to put your ideas in order. Think about the event you will relate in your descriptive writing. Use the sequence chart on this page to list the events in order.

Lesson 6 The Writing Process: Descriptive Writing

Draft

Now, it is time to write a first draft of your descriptive writing. Write your draft on this page. Look back at your sequence chart on page 96 whenever you need to. As you write, don't worry about misspelling words or getting every word exactly right. Just get your main ideas down in sentences and in order.

_____

_____

_____

_____

_____

_____

_____

_____

_____

_____

_____

_____

Write an idea for a title here. It is okay if it changes later.

Title: _____

Lesson 6 The Writing Process: Descriptive Writing

Revise

You worked hard to put your ideas on paper. You must now imagine that someone else wrote it. You must read your own work as if you have never seen it before. This is a hard job. But if you look at the writing with "new eyes," you are more likely to spot mistakes or problems.

Answer the questions below about your draft. If you answer "no" to any of these questions, those are the areas that might need improvement. Feel free to make marks on your draft so you know what needs more work.

- Did you keep your audience in mind? Did you include details that will interest them and that they will understand?
- Did you make your first sentence especially interesting so that readers will want to continue reading?
- Did you tell events in order? Did you use time-order words to make it clear when events happened?
- Did you use spatial words to show where things are?
- Did you use sense words? To how many of your readers' senses did you appeal?
- Did you use sentences of different lengths and styles to keep your writing interesting?

Read your draft again and underline words that tell how something looked, sounded, smelled, felt, or tasted. Is there one in every sentence? Are there just a few? Look carefully to see where you could add descriptive words to make your description stronger. Here is how Kathy changed a sentence in her draft.

<u>After the concert, the crowd was ~~loud~~ roaring.</u>

Lesson 6 The Writing Process: Descriptive Writing

Write the revision of your first draft below. As you revise, remember to make sure your order is clear and your description appeals to readers' senses.

_____

_____

_____

_____

_____

_____

_____

_____

_____

_____

_____

_____

_____

_____

If you need to change your title, write the new title below.

Title: _____

Lesson 6 The Writing Process: Descriptive Writing

Proofread

It is best to proofread for just one kind of error at a time. First, read through your passage once for capital letters. Read it again for end punctuation. Then, read it again for spelling. Here is a checklist to help you as you proofread your revised descriptive writing.

_____ Each sentence begins with a capital letter.

_____ Each sentence ends with the correct punctuation (period, question mark, or exclamation point).

_____ Each sentence states a complete thought.

_____ All words are spelled correctly.

_____ Each paragraph begins with an indented sentence.

When proofreaders work, they use certain symbols. Using these symbols makes their job easier. They will make your job easier, too.

- three little lines under a letter mean that something should be capitalized. Write the capitalized letter above it.

- If there is a period missing, do this.

- Can you insert a question mark like this?

- Don't forget your exclamation points!

- Fix misspelled words like this.

- Make this mark (¶) to show where to indent a paragraph.

Use these symbols as you proofread your descriptive writing. Remember to read your writing out loud. Sometimes it is easier to catch mistakes when reading out loud.

Lesson 6 The Writing Process: Descriptive Writing

Publish

Write a final copy of your personal narrative below. Write carefully and neatly so that there are no mistakes.

_____

_____

_____

_____

_____

_____

_____

_____

_____

_____

_____

_____

_____

_____

_____

Chapter 6
Lesson 1 A Story Line

A **story** tells about made-up people or animals. They are the **characters** in the story.

A story has a **setting** telling where and when the action takes place.

A story has a **plot**, or series of events, with a problem that needs to be solved.

An interesting **beginning**, a **middle**, and **end** make a story fun to read.

Describing words tell about the characters, setting, and events.

Read this story. Think about what happens at the beginning, in the middle, and at the end.

Max's Message

Today was Max's teacher's birthday, and Max woke up late. He scrambled around the house to get ready, brushing his teeth while pulling on his white socks. He grabbed a fresh apple from the kitchen on his way to the bus stop. He made it to the bus stop just as the bright yellow school bus was pulling up.

After Max hung up his red winter coat, he sat down at his desk in the middle of the room. Max then realized that he had forgotten Ms. Emery's birthday card at home. He hadn't put it in his backpack last night, and he had forgotten to grab it from the kitchen table on his way out. What was he going to do?

It was too cold outside to have recess, so Ms. Emery brought out the art supplies, and the students spent their recess drawing and writing. Max drew a huge birthday cake, with glowing candles and five layers. He wrote his name and took it up to Ms. Emery.

"Happy birthday, Ms. Emery," Max said.

Lesson 1 A Story Line

Answer these questions about "Max's Message." Look back at the story on page 102 if you need to.

Who are the characters in the story?

_____   _____

The action takes place in two settings. What are they?

_____   _____

What is the problem that Max has to solve?

_____

What happens at the beginning, in the middle, and at the end of the story?

Beginning	Middle	End

How does the writer describe the apple and the school bus? Find these and other describing words. List them here.

_____   _____

_____   _____

_____   _____

Lesson 2 Tell Me a Story

Do you like stories about dragons? Maybe you prefer stories with animals that talk. Or, maybe your favorite characters are from the planet Jupiter. Stories like these are called **fantasy**. Their characters could not be real or the events could not actually happen.

List some stories or books you have read that are fantasies:

_____   _____

_____   _____

What kind of fantasy would you like to write? Will you set it in a city in space or under the ocean? Maybe your main character has a special power of some sort. Let your imagination go and write down a couple of fantasy story ideas here.

Fantasy idea #1

Character(s): _____

Setting: _____

Plot: _____

_____

Fantasy idea #2

Character(s): _____

Setting: _____

Plot: _____

_____

Lesson 2 Tell Me a Story

Stories that include normal people who live on Earth are called **realistic**. Though their characters come from a writer's imagination, they could be real, and the events could actually happen.

List some stories or books you have read that are realistic:

_____   _____

_____   _____

What kind of realistic story would you like to write? Will it be about something funny that happens to an ordinary kid or a lost dog trying to find its way home? Realistic stories require just as much imagination as fantasies do. Jot down some realistic story ideas here.

Realistic story idea #1

Character(s): _____

Setting: _____

Plot: _____

_____

Realistic idea #2

Character(s): _____

Setting: _____

Plot: _____

_____

Lesson 3 Make Your Characters Speak

Dialogue is the conversation between characters in a story. When a writer uses dialogue in a story, the characters seem more real. Here is what dialogue looks like.

> "Has anyone seen Tippy?" Sharon asked. Her parents both shook their heads.
> "No, I haven't seen him, dear," said Dad.
> "Not since supper time," agreed Mom.
> Sharon swallowed. "I think he's lost," she squeaked, trying not to cry.

Take a closer look at a line of dialogue.

Quotation marks go before and after the speaker's exact words.

"No, I haven't seem him, dear," said Dad.

A **comma** separates the speaker's words from the tag line. It goes inside the ending quotation mark.

The **tag line** tells who is speaking.

Dialogue should sound like real people talking. An eight-year-old character should sound like a kid. A king should sound like a king. It wouldn't seem right to have a king say, "Hi, buddy. What's up?" would it? A king would probably say, "Hello, young man. How are you today?"

Write a line of dialogue for each character below. Make sure it sounds right based on the information about the character. Remember to use quotation marks, tag lines, and commas.

Mom, an important businesswoman: _____

_____

A young child who is lost in a store: _____

_____

Lesson 3 Make Your Characters Speak

Dialogue tells us more than what characters say. We learn about characters both by what they say and how they say it. We also learn about a character from what other characters say about him or her. Dialogue keeps readers interested and moves the story along.

Read the following lines of dialogue. Then, answer the questions.

> "Did you see a book lying on my desk, Mary?" asked Charles.
> "Why would I take your old book?" Mary challenged.
> "Because you would do anything to have something to read," Charles answered.
> Mary snorted, "Well, I can't help it if I don't have any money."
> Charles looked at Mary a long time. "Just give it back to me when you're done."

What do you know about Charles from these few lines of dialogue?

_____

_____

_____

What do you know about Mary? _____

_____

What do you know about the setting? _____

_____

What do you know about the plot? What do you think might happen next?

_____

_____

_____

Lesson 4 Make up a Simile

Sometimes, the goal of writing is to create a picture for the reader. One way to create a vivid picture is to use a **simile**. In a simile, two things that are not alike are compared, using the word *like* or *as*. The first sentence in the paragraph below is a simile. It compares snow to a blanket. What kind of picture does it create in your mind?

> Snow lay on the field like a blanket. Underneath it, mice scurried in their grassy tunnels. They were happy and safe underneath the warm covering.

Here is another simile. What pictures does it create for you?

> In their burrow, the mice snuggled together. They fit together like puzzle pieces, side to side and end to end.

In this simile, how mice snuggle together is compared to how puzzle pieces fit together. Adding the simile in the second sentence creates a vivid picture.

Some similes are very common. They usually involve comparing the color of something to the color of something else.

Her hair was *as black as coal*.

The tree's yellow leaves glowed *like flames*.

Try some similes on your own. Complete each simile with at least one word that creates a picture in your mind.

My face turned as red as _____

The old man's hair was as white as _____

The storm clouds rolled in like _____

Lesson 4 Make up a Simile

Similes do not always deal with color. They might relate to how something looks, sounds, feels, or tastes. Here are some more examples.

The little mouse looked *as soft as velvet*.

Her ears were *like little saucers* perched atop her head.

The snap of the trap was *like an explosion*. Mice scattered everywhere.

Remember, similes are all about creating images. Use your senses and your imagination and create some great images. Remember that you must use *like* or *as* in your comparison.

Write a simile in which you compare some detail about an animal to something else. Here is an example.

The frightened cat stopped; its tail stuck up like an antenna.

Write a simile about a sound.

_____

Write a simile about a texture or how something feels.

_____

Write a simile about how something looks.

_____

Write another simile about an object in the room around you.

_____

Lesson 5 Tell a Tall Tale

A **tall tale** is a special kind of story. In addition to made-up characters, it uses humor and exaggeration to tell its story. Exaggeration is when a writer stretches the truth and makes things larger, smaller, stronger, or different from how they really are. Here are some examples of exaggeration.

The wind blew so hard that the house tipped over.

My sister made such a fuss that they must have heard her in China.

Like a simile, exaggeration creates pictures for readers. With exaggeration, though, the picture is usually funny and often ridiculous.

Use exaggeration to complete these sentences.

Last winter it was so cold that _____

My turtle can run as fast as _____

He snored so loud, it sounded like _____

Jordan is so tall that _____

I felt so weak I couldn't even _____

It was so quiet you could hear _____

On Your Own
Exaggerations are fun to write and fun to draw. Complete this sentence.

Super Girl is so strong that she can _____

_____.

What picture does this bring to mind? Draw it on a separate sheet of paper. Then, write the sentence below the picture. Write more exaggerations and draw pictures. Make a book of exaggerations to share with your friends.

Lesson 5 Tell a Tall Tale

Now, think about writing a tall tale. Most tall tales involve a series of unusual events. The main character solves his or her problem with amazing cleverness or sometimes just incredibly good luck. Create a main character for your tall tale. Write some ideas here about your character. Remember to exaggerate how the character looks or acts.

Character's name: _____

How the character looks: _____

_____

What the character does or can do: _____

_____

Now, think about some unusual events. What kind of trouble does your character have? How does your character get out of trouble? List the main events of your tall tale below.

Character's problem

How character solves problem

How the story ends

Lesson 5 Tell a Tall Tale

Review the ideas about your character and his or her problems and solutions. Now, write a first draft of your tall tale here. Remember to introduce your character at the beginning, give your character a problem to try to solve in the middle, and show how the problem is solved at the end.

_____

_____

_____

_____

_____

_____

_____

_____

_____

_____

Questions to Ask About a Tall Tale

Does it have a beginning, middle, and an end?
Does its character have a problem? Does the character solve the problem?
Does it use exaggeration? Is it funny?
Does the language create pictures for your readers?

Lesson 6 The Writing Process: Story

Writing a story can take you into a different world or help you express your ideas about your own world. First, review the steps of the writing process.

Prewrite: Choose a topic. Collect ideas. Make lists or charts. Organize ideas.

Draft: Write ideas down on paper in sentences.

Revise: Fix mistakes in draft. Add details. Change things around to make the writing better. Rewrite the sentences.

Proofread: Check for final mistakes in spelling, capitalization, and punctuation.

Publish: Make a final, error-free copy. Share with readers.

Prewrite

Stories can be completely different, but they all have certain features.

- A story tells about made-up **characters**—people, animals, or both.
- A story has a **setting** that tells where and when the action takes place.
- A story has a **plot** that includes a problem that needs to be solved.
- An interesting **beginning, middle**, and **end** make a story fun to read.
- **Describing words** tell about the characters, setting, and events.

Look at the story ideas you developed on pages 104 and 105. Choose one of those ideas and begin to explore it here.

_____

_____

_____

_____

NAME _____

Lesson 6 The Writing Process: Story

Now, work on the character of your story. Use this idea web to record details about how he or she looks, acts, speaks, and so on.

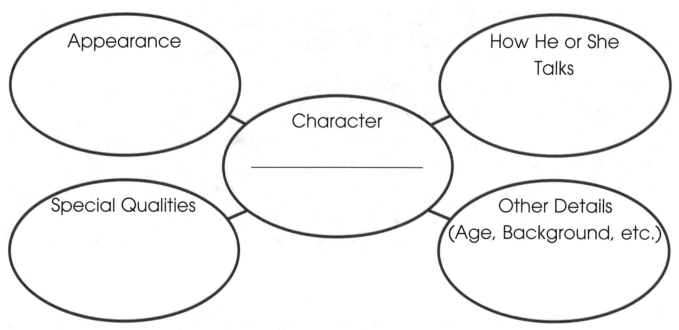

Answer these questions about your setting and plot.

What is the setting of your story? Consider these issues: place or location, season, time of day, weather conditions.

_____

_____

What is the character's problem?

_____

_____

What does the character do to try to solve the problem? Does it take more than one try?

_____

_____

Lesson 6 The Writing Process: Story

So far, you have chosen a topic and collected ideas. Now, it is time to put your ideas in order. Think about the story you are about to tell. Use the story map on this page to list the important parts of your story.

Character(s)

_____

Setting

_____

Problem

_____

Plot: Beginning

_____

_____

_____

Plot: Middle

_____

_____

_____

Plot: End

_____

_____

_____

Lesson 6 The Writing Process: Story

Draft

Write your story on this page, using your story map on page 115. As you write, don't worry about misspelled words or perfect punctuation. Just write your ideas down in sentences that are in order.

_____

_____

_____

_____

_____

_____

_____

_____

_____

_____

_____

_____

_____

_____

_____

Write an idea for a title here. You can change it later if you wish.

Title: _____

Lesson 6 The Writing Process: Story

Revise

As you begin to revise your own draft, try to pretend that you are reading the work for the very first time. This will help you find any mistakes.

Answer the questions below about your draft. If you answer "no" to any of these questions, those are the areas that might need improvement. Feel free to make marks on your draft, so you know what needs more work.

- Did you give details about an interesting character and a setting?
- Did you include a problem and a solution in your plot?
- Did you tell events in an order that made sense?
- Did you create pictures in your readers' minds with well-chosen words?
- Did you use dialogue to help readers learn about characters and to move the story forward?
- Did you enclose characters' words in quotation marks?
- Did you describe how things look, sound, smell, feel, and taste?
- Did you use sentences of different lengths and styles?

Kristi began to write a story. Here are some examples of punctuating dialogue. Notice how the tag lines, quotation marks, and commas are used.

"Where did you go for so long?" Ma called when she saw Pa.

Pa put down the sack he was carrying. It was about the size of a tractor. "Well, there weren't any potatoes in town," he answered.

"So, what did you do?" asked Ma, curiously.

Pa spoke proudly, "Well, I just dug some up along the way back home."

Ma was shocked. "You don't mean you dug up Mr. Spencer's potatoes!" she cried.

Lesson 6 The Writing Process: Story

Write the revision of your first draft here. As you revise, remember to make your characters say things that sound natural.

_____

_____

_____

_____

_____

_____

_____

_____

_____

_____

_____

_____

_____

_____

Are you still happy with your title? If not, write a new title below.

Title: _____

Lesson 6 The Writing Process: Story

Proofread

It is best to proofread for just one kind of error at a time. First, read through your story once for capital letters. Read it again for end punctuation. Then, read it again for spelling. Here is a checklist to help you as you proofread your revised story.

> _____ Each sentence begins with a capital letter.
> _____ Each sentence ends with the correct punctuation (period, question mark, or exclamation point).
> _____ Dialogue is punctuated correctly.
> _____ Each sentence states a complete thought.
> _____ All words are spelled correctly. (If you're not sure, check a dictionary.)

When proofreaders work, they use certain symbols. Using these symbols makes their job easier. They will make your job easier, too.

> - T̲ three little lines under a letter mean that something should be capitalized. Write the capitalized letter above it.
>
> - Write in a missing end mark like this: ⊙ ? !
>
> - Add a comma and quotation marks like this " he said.
>
> - Fix misspelled words like this.

Use these symbols as you proofread your story. Remember to read your writing out loud. Sometimes it is easier to catch mistakes when reading out loud.

Lesson 6 The Writing Process: Story

Publish

Write a final copy of your story below. Write carefully and neatly so that there are no mistakes. Then, think of ways to share your story.

_____

_____

_____

_____

_____

_____

_____

_____

_____

_____

_____

_____

_____

_____

_____

Writer's Handbook

Writing Basics

Sentences are a writer's building blocks. To be a good writer, one must first be a good sentence writer. A sentence always begins with a capital letter.

> **He** walked around the block.

A sentence must always tell a complete thought. It has a subject and a predicate.

> Complete Sentence: He lives around the corner.
> Incomplete Sentence: The block where he lives.

A sentence always ends with an end mark. There are three kinds of end marks. A sentence that tells something ends with a period.

> He walked around the block.

A sentence that asks something ends with a question mark.

> Did he walk around the block**?**

A sentence that shows excitement or fear ends with an exclamation point.

> He ran all the way around the block**!**

Punctuation can be a writer's road map.

End marks on sentences show whether a sentence is a statement, a question, or an exclamation.

Commas help keep ideas clear.

> In a list or series: I saw sea stars, crabs, and seals at the beach.
> In a compound sentence: I wanted a closer look, but the crab crawled away.
> After an introductory phrase or clause: Later that day, a storm blew up.
> To separate a speech tag: I called to Mom, "It's really getting windy!"
> "I hope it doesn't rain," she said.

Quotation marks show the exact words that a speaker says. Quotation marks enclose the speaker's words and the punctuation marks that go with the words.

> "Does it matter?" Neil remarked. "We're already wet."
> "I'd rather be wet from below than from above," said Dad.
> "Be careful!" Mom yelled. "Those waves are getting big!"

Writer's Handbook

The Writing Process

When writers write, they take certain steps. Those steps make up the writing process.

Step 1: Prewrite

First, writers choose a topic. Then, they collect and organize ideas or information. They might write their ideas in a list or make a chart and begin to put their ideas in some kind of order.

Mariko is going to write about her neighborhood. She put her ideas in a web.

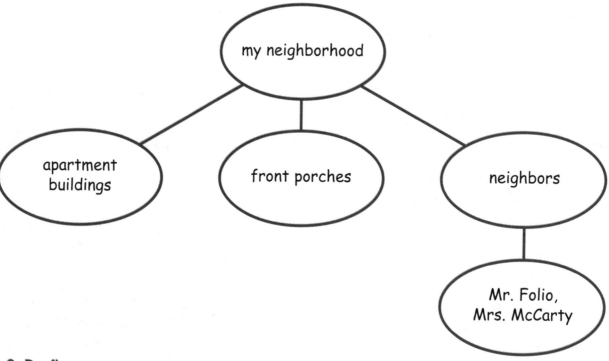

Step 2: Draft

Next, writers put their ideas on paper in a first draft. Writers know that there might be mistakes in this first draft. That's okay. Here is Mariko's first draft.

_____ Brick apartment houses are all around me. I live in tallest one. Across the street is the shortest. I like to think of the windows as eyes. and the front porches are the mouths People go in and out. Mr. Folio, my favorite neighbor, sits and sings songs. Mrs. McCarty pretends to shake a rug out the window but she is really listening to Mr. Folio.

Writer's Handbook

Step 3: Revise

Then, writers change or fix their first draft. They might decide to move ideas around, add information, or take out words or sentences that don't belong. Here are Mariko's changes.

> Brick apartment houses are all around me. I live in the tallest one. ~~Across the street is the shortest.~~ I like to think of the windows as eyes. and the front porches are the mouths People go in and out. Mr. Folio, my favorite neighbor, sits on his porch and sings Italian songs.
> In the evening, Mrs. McCarty pretends to shake a rug out the window but she is really listening to
> Mr. Folio.

Step 4: Proofread

Writers usually write a new copy so their writing is neat. Then, they look again to make sure everything is correct. They look for mistakes in their sentences. Mariko found several more mistakes when she proofread her work.

> Brick apartment houses are all around me. I live in the tallest one. I like to think of the windows as eyes and the front porches are the mouths. People go in and out. Mr. Folio, my favorite neighbor, sits on his porch and sings Italian songs. In the evening, Mrs. McCarty pretends to shake a rug out the window but she is really listening to
> Mr. Folio.

Step 5: Publish

Finally, writers make a final copy that has no mistakes. They might choose to add pictures and create a book. Then, they are ready to publish their writing. They might choose to read their writing out loud or have a friend read it.

Writer's Handbook

Personal Narrative

In a personal narrative, a writer writes about something she has done or seen. It might tell about something funny, sad, or unusual. A personal narrative can be about anything, as long as the writer is telling about one of his or her own experiences. Here is the final version of Mariko's paragraph about her neighborhood.

Describing words help readers "see" or "hear" what is happening.	

Brick apartment houses are all around me. I live in the tallest one. I like to think of the windows as eyes and front porches as mouths. People go in and out. Mr. Folio, my favorite neighbor, sits on his porch and sings Italian songs. In the evening, Mrs. McCarty pretends to shake a rug out the window, but she is really listening to Mr. Folio.

The words *me* and *I* show that the writer is part of the action.

A time word tells when something happens.

The writer stayed on topic. All of the sentences give information about Mariko's neighborhood.

Stories

Writers write about made-up things. They might write about people or animals. The story might seem real, or it might seem fantastic, or unreal. Here is a story that Mariko wrote. It has both human and animal characters in it. The animals speak, so Mariko's story is not realistic.

The story has a beginning, a middle, and an end.

In the Neighborhood

It is nearly sunrise, and the neighborhood is waking up. Windows glow where the early birds prepare breakfast. Bacon sizzles in the Hooper kitchen, and the smell draws a hungry crowd.

In the corner, eight furry paws scramble through the crack between the wall and the baseboard. They pause at the corner of the wastebasket, then scamper to the refrigerator. Blue fuzzy slippers come quickly forward and stamp on the floor. "Go away, you critters!" The critters huddle deeper in the darkness. Four black eyes watch for crumbs to fall. Two long tails twitch with excitement.

Mrs. Hooper's slippers scuff across the floor. "It's ready!" she calls upstairs. In a moment, Mr. Hooper's heavy work boots thump down the stairs. *Scuff-thump, Scuff-thump*, the people go into the other room.

"Now, it's our turn." smiles Velvet.

Her brother Flannel nods and shrugs. "It's a dirty job, but someone has to do it." And he and his sister go to work, clearing the floor of crumbs.

The first paragraph establishes the setting.

Sensory words help readers visualize what is happening.

Time and order words keep ideas in order.

This story is written in third-person point of view. So, words such as *he*, *she*, *her*, *his*, and *they* refer to the characters.

The story includes dialogue, or conversation among characters.

Writer's Handbook

Descriptive Writing

When writers describe, they might tell about an object, a place, or an event. They use sensory words so that readers can see, hear, smell, feel, or taste whatever is being described. In this example of descriptive writing, Mariko compared her old bedroom with her new bedroom.

The writer uses the whole-to-whole comparison method. She describes one whole room in the first paragraph, and the other room in the second paragraph.

> My bedroom in our old apartment was green. It was a nice grassy green, and it always made me think of a forest. My bed was in the left corner, between the two windows. The wall straight ahead was almost all shelves, where I kept my turtle collection, my books, and all my other stuff. My yellow beanbag chair and the closet were on the right side of the room.
>
> My new bedroom is blue. I like to think of it as sky blue. On the left side of the room is one big window. I put my beanbag chair right beside the window. Straight ahead is my bed. On the right is a built-in bookshelf and the closet door.

Sensory details help readers visualize the scene.

The writer organizes details from side to side. She first tells what is on the left, then straight ahead, then on the right.

Informational Writing

When writers write to inform, they present information about a topic. Informational writing is nonfiction. It is not made up; it contains facts.

Mariko interviewed her neighbor, Mr. Folio. Then, she wrote about what she learned. Here is one of her paragraphs.

Mariko states her main idea in a topic sentence. It is the first sentence of the paragraph.

Transition words connect ideas.

> My neighbor, Mr. Folio, has lived in the same apartment building all his life. His parents and his grandparents lived there, too. In fact, his grandparents were the first people to move into the building in 1921. He remembers his grandmother telling about how new and shiny the doorknobs and the stair railings were. Mr. Folio's grandparents lived on the top floor because his grandfather liked the view. Later, his parents lived on the fourth floor because that was what was available at the time. Now, Mr. Folio lives on the first floor. He says he likes to see what is going on in the neighborhood.

These sentences contain details that support the main idea.

Writer's Handbook

Explanatory (or How-to) Writing

Writers explain how to do things. They might write about how to play a game, create an art project, or follow a recipe. Mariko has written instructions for a marble game that she plays with her sister.

> **Mariko's Marbles**
>
> First, you need 20 small marbles, two shooter marbles, and someone to play with. Choose a square of sidewalk that doesn't have very many cracks or bumps in it. Roll the small marbles onto the square. Then, players take turns using their shooters to try to knock marbles out of the square. Each player gets two tries per turn. Players may knock out only one marble at a time. If a player knocks out more than one marble, the player must put back all of her knocked-out marbles. Finally, when all 20 marbles have been knocked out of the square, the player with the most marbles is the winner.

The steps are all in order, starting with the items needed to play the game.

Order words help readers keep the steps in order.

Clear words help readers understand the instructions.

Persuasive Writing

In persuasive writing, writers try to make readers think, feel, or act in a certain way. Persuasive writing shows up in newspaper and magazine articles, letters to the editor, business letters, and in advertisements, of course. Mariko's mom has written a letter to the editor of the local newspaper.

> Dear Editor:
>
> I used to be proud of my neighborhood. The streets used to look nice, and people cared about keeping them that way. Now, however, the sidewalks on 41st Street are terribly cracked and broken, and the city has no plans to fix them. In some places, it is not even safe to walk. The older people in the neighborhood have to walk in the street to get to the grocery store. Can't the city repair the sidewalks? It would feel good to be proud and safe in my neighborhood again.
>
> F. Torunaga

The writer begins by stating some opinions.

The writer uses an emotional appeal to persuade readers to agree with her.

The writer states some facts to lend support to her opinions.

The writer includes a specific request for action.

Writer's Handbook

Friendly Letters

Writers write friendly letters to people they know. They might share news or ideas or request information. A friendly letter has four parts: the date, the greeting, the body, and the closing, which includes the signature. Here is a letter Mariko wrote to her grandfather.

Each word in the greeting begins with a capital letter.

There is always a comma after the person's name.

The date is in the upper, right corner.

September 2

Dear Grandfather,

We are all settled in our new apartment. I love my new bedroom. Dad says we can even paint some white puffy clouds on the ceiling. Then it really will seem like a sky-blue room.

The body of the letter gives information.

I like the neighbors, so far. Mr. Folio is my favorite. He lives in a building across the street. When there's nothing to do, I go sit on his front steps and visit. He can tell a story about almost everyone who passes by on the sidewalk.

I think you would like Mr. Folio. When are you and Grandmother going to come and visit? Soon, I hope.

Only the first word of the closing begins with a capital letter. There is always a comma after the closing.

Love as always,
Mariko

The writer signs his or her name.

Writer's Handbook

Business Letters

Writers write business letters to people or organizations with whom they are not familiar. Business letters usually involve a complaint or a request for information. Mariko needs information for a school report. She wrote a business letter to request information.

The heading includes the sender's address and the date.	764 41st Street Indianapolis, IN 46208 October 5, 2007

The inside address is the name and address of the recipient.

Monroe County Historical Society
202 E. 6th Street
Bloomington, IN 47402

Dear Monroe County Historical Society: ◄——— The greeting is followed by a colon.

The text of the letter is the body.

My class is studying state history this year. Each of us has chosen a county to study. I chose Monroe County because my grandparents live there.

On your Web site, I saw that you have a free pamphlet titled "Monroe County: Through the Years." Please send me one copy of that brochure. I have included an envelope with postage.

Thank you for your help with my report.

Sincerely,

Mariko Torunaga ——————— The closing is followed by a comma.

Mariko Torunaga

The sender always includes a signature.

Answer Key

Chapter 1

Lesson 1

Page 5
Animals and plants live in the desert.

Page 6
Answers will vary.

Lesson 2

Page 7
Circled titles:
Alex's Bad Day
Building for Tomorrow
School Days Return

Page 8
Titles will vary.

Lesson 3

Page 9
Circled titles:
A New Home for Turtle
Rainy Day Drawing

Page 10
Titles will vary.

Lesson 4

Page 11
Circled main ideas:
The games we play have been around
   for many years.
I got ready for school early.

Page 12
Main ideas will vary.

Lesson 5

Page 13
Circled errors:
cage My
week. best

Page 14
Paragraphs will vary.

Page 15
Paragraphs will vary.

Lesson 6

Page 16
Crossed-out sentences:
When I was little, I took dancing lessons.
Next week, I hope to have some flowers
   to plant.

Page 17
Crossed-out sentence:
I have a dress with lots of bright colors.
Paragraphs will vary.

Answer Key

Chapter 2

Lesson 1

Page 19
Order of steps, as shown:
Step 2: Draft
Step 4: Proofread
Step 1: Prewrite
Step 5: Publish
Step 3: Revise

Lesson 2

Page 20
Lists will vary.

Page 21
Lists will vary.

Lesson 3

Page 22
Lists will vary.

Page 23
Lists will vary.

Lesson 4

Page 25
Idea webs will vary.

Lesson 5

Page 26
Charts will vary.

Page 27
Charts will vary.

Lesson 6

Page 28
Time words and phrases will vary.
Sentences will vary.

Page 29
Circled transition words:
Then, Later

Underlined time words:
half an hour, the day, late
Sentences will vary.

Lesson 7

Page 30
Sentences and paragraphs will vary.

Page 31
Descriptions will vary.

Page 32
Descriptions will vary.

Lesson 8

Page 33
News articles will vary.

Page 34
Responses will vary.

Lesson 9

Page 35
Diagrams will vary.

Page 36
Diagrams and sentences will vary.

Lesson 10

Page 37
Stone Mountain is shorter than Rock Mountain.
Sal is sadder than Hal.
Hal is happier than Sal.

Page 38
Sentences will vary.
Tim is the shortest player.

Page 39
Kite 3 has the longest tail.
Kite 2 has the shortest tail.
Responses will vary.

Answer Key

Chapter 3

Lesson 1
Page 40
Journal entries will vary.

Page 41
Entries will vary.

Lesson 2
Page 42
Responses will vary.

Page 43
Paragraphs will vary.

Lesson 3
Page 44
Responses will vary.

Page 45

> July 6
>
> Dear Jennifer,
>   Thank you for your letter, dear. Fluffy is much better, now.
>   I remember seeing Fluffy with that napkin. I went to the kitchen right after that. I had the giggles, too!
>   Love,
>   Grandma

Lesson 4
Page 46
date
greeting
body
closing
Notes will vary.

Page 47
Letters will vary.

Lesson 5
Page 48
Responses will vary.

Page 49
Letters will vary.

Lesson 6
Page 51
Responses will vary.

Lesson 7
Page 52
Responses will vary.

Page 53
Responses will vary.

Page 54
Sequence charts will vary

Page 55
First drafts will vary.

Page 57
Revisions will vary.

page 59
Personal narratives will vary.

Answer Key

Chapter 4

Lesson 1

Page 60
sentence: <u>The storm</u> (came suddenly.)
fragment (missing a subject)
fragment (missing a predicate)

Page 61
run-on (corrected to: I heard a crash. It was up in the kitchen.)
run-on (corrected to: Mom went upstairs, but I stayed in the basement. OR Mom went upstairs. I stayed in the basement.)
sentence
run-on (corrected to: It was the cat, and he had knocked over a plant. OR It was the cat. He had knocked over a plant.)

Lesson 2

Page 63
<u>Tyler</u>
X <u>Popcorn</u>
X <u>Mrs. Kraft</u>
X <u>The mess</u>

Lesson 3

Page 64
Lists will vary.

Page 65
Lists will vary.

Lesson 4

Page 66
O
F
O

Page 67
Opinions and facts will vary.

Lesson 5

Page 68

Students should circle sentences 1 and 3.

Page 69
Lists will vary.

Lesson 6

Page 70
Instructions will vary.

Page 71
Instructions will vary.

Lesson 7

Page 72
(First,) go (down) this hallway. When you get to the (end,) turn (left.) Walk (past) the main office. (Then), the nurse's office is the (second) door on the (right.)

Page 73
Directions will vary.

Lesson 8

Page 74
Questions will vary.

Page 75
Questions will vary.

Lesson 9

Page 76
Possible topics will vary.

Page 77
Responses will vary.

Page 78
Chart entries will vary.

Page 79
First drafts will vary.

Page 81
Revised news stories will vary.

Page 83
Final news stories will vary.

Answer Key

Chapter 5

Lesson 1

Page 84
Listed items will vary.

Page 85
Paragraphs will vary.

Lesson 2

Page 86
Responses will vary.

Page 87
Riddles will vary.

Lesson 3

Page 88
Descriptions will vary.

Page 89
Paragraphs will vary.

Lesson 4

Page 90
Responses will vary.

Page 91
Descriptions will vary.

Lesson 5

Page 92
Descriptions will vary.

Page 93
Descriptions will vary.

Lesson 6

Page 94
Responses will vary.

Page 95
Responses will vary.

Page 96
Charts will vary.

Page 97
First drafts will vary.

Page 99
Revisions will vary.

Page 101
Final descriptions will vary.

Answer Key

Chapter 6

Lesson 1

Page 103
Max, Ms. Emery
Max's house, a classroom
He forgot Ms. Emery's birthday card at home.
Beginning: Max slept in and was almost late.
Middle: Max noticed that he forgot Ms. Emery's birthday card at home.
End: Max draws a birthday card for her.
"fresh apple," "bright yellow school bus"; Other descriptive words will vary.

Lesson 2

Page 104
Responses will vary.

Page 105
Responses will vary.

Lesson 3

Page 106
Dialogue will vary.

Page 107
Possible answers:
Charles may be older than Mary. Charles "has money."
Mary likes to read. She doesn't "have any money."
The setting is in a room with a desk.
The plot might have to do with Mary taking things that don't belong to her. It might have something to do with finding a way for Mary to get things to read. It might have to do with how Charles helps Mary.

Lesson 4

Page 108
Similes will vary.

Page 109
Similes will vary.

Lesson 5

Page 110
Sentences will vary.

Page 111
Responses will vary.

Page 112
Tall Tales will vary.

Lesson 6

Page 113
Story ideas will vary.

Page 114
Chart entries and responses will vary.

Page 115
Story map entries will vary.

Page 116
First drafts will vary.

Page 118
Revisions will vary.

Page 120
Final stories will vary.

Notes

Make Writing Exciting!

Motivating Lessons, Focused Activities on Specific Skills,
and Reproducible Patterns to Teach Essential Writing Techniques

by Kelly Gunzenhauser

illustrated by
Vanessa Countryman

Publisher
Key Education Publishing Company, LLC
Minneapolis, MN 55438
www.keyeducationpublishing.com

CONGRATULATIONS ON YOUR PURCHASE OF A KEY EDUCATION PRODUCT!

The editors at Key Education are former teachers who bring experience, enthusiasm, and quality to each and every product. Thousands of teachers have looked to the staff at Key Education for new and innovative resources to make their work more enjoyable and rewarding. We are committed to developing educational materials that will assist teachers in building a strong and developmentally appropriate curriculum for young children.

PLAN FOR GREAT TEACHING EXPERIENCES WHEN YOU USE EDUCATIONAL MATERIALS FROM KEY EDUCATION PUBLISHING COMPANY, LLC

About the Author

Kelly Gunzenhauser has a master's degree in English and taught writing at the college level. She has worked in educational publishing for eleven years and is the author of seven books for teachers and children, including Key Education's *Sequencing Cut-Up Paragraphs, Creating Curriculum Using Children's Picture Books, Reading for Details, Graphic Organizers That Help Struggling Learners, Let's Learn and Play!* and *Make Writing Exciting!* Kelly has two sons in preschool and spends her time playing and learning with them and volunteering at their school.

Acknowledgments

I would like to acknowledge the following people who contributed their research, advice, and ideas for this book: Sherrill B. Flora, Deborah Kitzman, Rachel Hoeing, and Ashley Anderson. I would also like to say a special thank you to my friend Garrett Fisch—a third grader and a very good writer—for his excellent suggestions and insight. K. G.

Dedication

To Eric

Credits
Author: Kelly Gunzenhauser
Publisher: Sherrill B. Flora
Illustrator: Vanessa Countryman
Editors: Debra Pressnall and Karen Seberg
Cover Design & Production: Annette Hollister-Papp
Page Design & Layout: Debra Pressnall
Cover Photographs: © Shutterstock, © Digital Vision, and © Brand X

Key Education welcomes manuscripts and product ideas from teachers. For a copy of our submission guidelines, please visit our Web site or send a self-addressed, stamped envelope to:

Key Education Publishing Company, LLC
Acquisitions Department
7309 West 112th Street
Minneapolis, Minnesota 55438

Standard Book Number: 978-1-602680-70-8
Make Writing Exciting!
Copyright © 2010 by Key Education Publishing Company, LLC
Minneapolis, Minnesota 55438

Printed in the USA • All rights reserved

Table of Contents

Teaching writing is no longer a new expectation for teachers; however, it can still be a difficult task. One reason is that there are so many kinds of writing. It can be hard to know what to teach, even within a set curriculum. Another reason is that, even with a rubric, teachers may not be sure if they are evaluating writing fairly. Still another reason is that being a good writer, just like being a good mathematician or a good athlete or a good surgeon or a good driver, does not come naturally to everyone. It can be difficult to feel that writing is a subject one has mastered well enough to teach. Teachers are constantly told to write with their students, but not all teachers use their spare time to "just write," and those who do often prefer to do it in private. Sitting down to write may not seem like a natural act to do in front of students. These are some of the issues addressed in *Make Writing Exciting!* All kinds of writing that teachers do (progress reports, forms, notes, etc.) are recognized in this book. There are many ideas for making writing lessons more interactive and more inviting to students with different learning levels and learning styles. Hopefully, using this book to supplement or build a writing curriculum will also have the effect of making writing time a fun and productive treat that students—and teachers—look forward to experiencing.

What kinds of writing skills are emphasized in this book? In addition to stories, reports, and essays, many other types of writing are valued in *Make Writing Exciting!* Lists, letters, directions, journals, forms, and writing across the curriculum are covered as well as other skills that students need to be better writers, such as word choice, writing good sentences, editing and proofreading, and all steps of the writing process. Also included in this book are suggestions for how to assess student writing and how to teach students to evaluate their own and others' writing.

In what order should I teach writing skills? Do I have to start at the beginning? You can use the chapters and skills in order to teach writing sequentially. Using the lessons consecutively does have the advantage of helping students construct a scaffold of skills. But, you may want to skip around depending on students' skill levels and the existing writing curriculum. It is fine to choose any form of writing as a starting point. It may also be necessary to revisit easier skills to build student confidence or to jump around as teachable moments come up, using individual activities to reinforce these skills.

I teach children with special needs. Is this an appropriate book for me? Absolutely! Students with special needs require more support, more practice, a slower pace, and fresh approaches to help them write to the best of their abilities. Throughout this book are ideas for instructional support that these students need as you build their skills and confidence. See pages 6 and 7 for general tips and suggestions that will help students with special needs get the most out of their writing lessons.

What supplies do I need for the lessons in this book? In addition to pencils and paper, consider providing a notebook with pockets for each child to use as a journal, "fun" writing paper (wrapping paper, construction paper, etc.), colored pencils, crayons, markers, other art supplies, at least one tape recorder, headphones, and a computer and word processing program (if possible). A few activities call for special materials.

But, I DON'T write every day! How do I make writing a habit? First of all, yes, you do—probably quite a lot. You write e-mails to friends, family, and your students' parents; you write lesson plans; you write notes to students, grocery lists, calendar updates, and maybe even notes to tuck in your own child's lunch box. Writing is not all about essays or stories. Once you make up your mind to value all writing in the classroom, you can help students see writing as a part of everyday life just by doing the writing you already have to do.

I dread writing time and my students do, too. How can I fix that? Again, consider the writing you are already doing—you write more than you think. Next, make writing a treat so that you do not dread it so much, and students will follow your lead. Use these guidelines to make writing something to look forward to.

- Integrate writing activities into show-and-tell, art, math, science, playground time, and so on. Adding writing to other activities gives students extra practice and gives the writing "a point." Suggestions for this are listed in each chapter.

- Combine writing with any activity you and the class enjoy. Offer special privileges during writing time: share a special snack, show a film and let students respond to it in writing, or let students write with watercolor markers or colored-ink pens.

- Change the atmosphere during writing time. Play music and dim the lighting. Let students write outside or on the floor, trade desks, or even take turns sitting at your

desk as you walk around the room. If they make a big deal about these changes, that's great—tell them to write about how they feel and why they think you have made the changes. They may even have their own suggestions!

- Make the classroom writing atmosphere quiet, but not too quiet. Silent periods often feel too much like testing periods. Plus, many students work better with a little background noise. Of course, you will want to recreate a testing atmosphere during some writing periods so that students take the testing atmosphere in stride when they eventually complete a standardized writing test.

- Do what makes it better for you. Students detect how their teachers feel about things. Analyze exactly what you do not enjoy about the writing period; then, produce changes that will make you happier. For example, if you do not relish keeping a journal but force yourself to journalize during in-class writing time, stop keeping a journal and work on other writing that you need to do.

- Celebrate writing during the publishing stage. Letting students help decide how they want to celebrate will motivate them to do their best. Look at Chapter 12: Proud to Be Published for ideas.

As the title suggests, the activities in this book are designed to make writing a fun time for students. But, the teacher needs to have fun, too. Do not forget to address your own needs. What do you need to enjoy writing? Whatever it is, do it for yourself. If you enjoy writing time and look forward to it, your enthusiasm will carry over to your students.

Teaching Students with Special Needs

Especially in inclusion classrooms, students may have vastly differing abilities and may move at very different paces. The personal success of students with special needs may be great, even as their scores on standardized writing tests may be poor. Your job is to address all types of writing success as much as possible. Consider these points as you teach students with special needs, and indeed, all students.

- Some students may have difficulty with the fine motor skills needed to write. Invite those students to draw, "drite," dictate as you write, tape-record their thoughts, type, or do whatever it takes. (To strengthen fine motor skills, let students complete mazes and dot-to-dot puzzles, trace pictures or letters, finger paint letters and words, etc.)

- Offer the options listed above to all students. Students with special needs are less likely to feel singled out if they and classmates are using the same methods to get their thoughts on paper (or recorded), plus all students will benefit from a variety of fine motor exercises.

- Some students need a lot of practice sessions to become comfortable using a new strategy or element in their writing. Let those students have many opportunities to practice each new writing element or strategy. When they get stuck, help them problem solve. You might ask, "What have we tried before that could help you write longer sentences?" "What are some other ways that you can add more details to your story?"

- Cater to different learning styles so that all learners can approach writing in a way that is comfortable for them.

To engage tactile/kinesthetic learners, have students:

- ➤ Move to different writing stations. (Be sure a handwriting chart is posted in each location or is part of the student's writing folder to reduce any anxiety in remembering how to write specific letters. It is important for some students to be able to touch the chart when looking for a certain letter.)
- ➤ Write standing at a table or sitting on the floor if that makes them comfortable.
- ➤ Eat crunchy snacks or chew gum while writing.
- ➤ Do a short routine of movements before writing, like shaking out hands or stretching.
- ➤ Type their work if it is short by using a word processing program. (Some students with dysgraphia may also struggle to learn keyboarding skills and need to use specialized technology tools when typing their text.)

To engage auditory learners, have students:

➤ Write about what you read to them immediately after you have shared a book. Break up the task by writing page by page or let them summarize very short stories.

➤ Dictate stories for others to transcribe so that they are talking while someone else is doing the writing.

➤ Ask each other interview questions and respond in writing.

➤ Read their own writing aloud as they record themselves; then, listen to their recordings.

➤ Sing their writing or write song lyrics.

To engage visual learners, have students:

➤ Use different media for writing, including computers.

➤ Combine art and text by making letter collages, creating pictures made of tiny letters, coloring letter outlines, and illustrating their stories and others' stories.

➤ Write birthday stories on wrapping paper.

• Students on the autism spectrum or who have attention deficit hyperactivity disorder (ADHD) require extra effort on your part to keep their attention. Accomplish this by providing activities in a variety of lengths. Writing is a good transitional activity, so use short writing activities during transition time when you can.

• If a student in your class has a paraprofessional or shadow, let the shadow act as a scribe while the student dictates the text.

• Have the student first draw a picture about the topic if words do not flow easily.

• Assign many genres of writing, including notes, lists, order forms, and journals.

• Allow a student to write in a study carrel or work cubby to reduce visual distractions. These special work areas can be decorated with handwriting charts, encouraging messages that other students have written, and word lists to inspire writing ideas. The space can also be personalized with small student-drawn posters.

Structuring Writing Lessons

This book offers lessons on formats (like letters and lists), elements (like prepositional phrases and more colorful language), strategies (like brainstorming and reading paragraphs backwards to evaluate individual sentences), and skills (like combining sentences and finding main ideas). Most of the lessons and reproducibles in this book will fit into any lesson plan or curriculum you already have. Use the **Writing Lesson Planner** reproducible (page 9) to create great student writing experiences.

Lesson Structure Ideas

This is a practical, easy lesson structure to follow. Most of the lessons and reproducibles in this book fit into this structure. However, you know what your students need to understand new formats, elements, strategies, and skills, so modify these steps accordingly.

1. First, define each new format, element, strategy, or skill. Name it, tell what it is, give examples, and then ask students to do the same. Most importantly, tell why this element or strategy can help make their writing better. For example, when teaching lists, let the class describe the features of a list as you make a list of their descriptions. Students can then brainstorm kinds of lists that people make.

2. Let students practice finding the format, element, strategy, or skill in others' writings. Again, when teaching lists, let them look for lists in their textbooks or assign them to bring in lists from home that their parents have made. Many of the reproducibles and exercises in this book provide opportunities for practice in recognizing different formats, elements, strategies, and skills.

3. Finally, encourage students to practice using the new format, element, strategy, or skill in their own written work. Following the above example, they can make their own lists at this time.

4. Have students record names and descriptions of formats, elements, strategies, and skills you have taught. The listings will prompt them to combine new skills to improve their own writing. In the backs of their journals, have them write the name of the new format, element, or strategy; a brief definition; and a line or two about when to use it.

5. Use copies of the **Writing Lesson Planner** to help you design your writing lessons. Write names of activities and their page numbers in the boxes. You may also wish to include in your notes how much time to allot for each part of the lesson. Exercises from other resources that you have already used can also be referenced here. As you complete successful lessons, punch holes in each page and store it to create your own tried-and-tested writing lesson book.

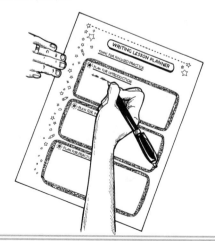

WRITING LESSON PLANNER

TOPIC FOR FOCUSED PRACTICE

 PLAN FOR INTRODUCTION

 PLAN FOR FINDING EXAMPLES

 PLAN FOR PRACTICE

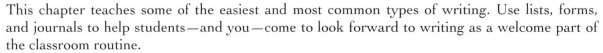

First Writing

This chapter teaches some of the easiest and most common types of writing. Use lists, forms, and journals to help students—and you—come to look forward to writing as a welcome part of the classroom routine.

Lists

Lists are a great first writing assignment. They require no grammar and little formatting and can be used later on to generate writing ideas. Brainstorming is really just a list, no matter what form it takes. For the class's first writing lessons, find time each day for students to make different lists using the following writing activities and reproducibles. Allow students to read their lists aloud when possible. Students with special needs and beginning writers may need to type or dictate their answers.

Special Tips for Lists

- Let students make lists on notepads designed for list making. Even if the lines are not the exact size needed for young students, they will enjoy making lists that look like the ones their parents make.

- Tailor the paper to the list. Let students write grocery lists on grocery bags, gift wish lists on holiday or birthday wrapping paper, and food lists on paper plates.

- If you have access to a computer with a word processing program, show students how to use the automatic bulleting and numbering features as they type their lists. Frequently changing the choice of fonts and colors will encourage them to type more often to see what the new fonts and colors look like.

- Allow students to use tiny stickers in place of bullet points on their lists. This adds decoration and helps students improve fine motor skills.

- To help differentiate items, let students alternate between two pencil colors on their lists or highlight every other item. This will help each child keep his place in the text when he reads one of his lists aloud.

List Reproducibles

- Provide copies of the **Decorative Blank List** reproducible (page 19) when students are generating short lists. Each student can neatly copy her list on the **Journal Page** reproducible (page 20) to publish it or use this page when compiling a long list.

- Use the **ABC Journal** reproducibles (pages 21 and 22) to have students write alphabetized lists. Write the name of the assignment at the top and copy it for students. They can write alphabetized lists of classmates' names, animals, foods, or items in any other category you are studying.

- Use the **Write-On Plate** reproducible (page 25) to inspire lists about food. Students can list yummy foods, yucky foods, items on a dinner table, foods prepared for a holiday meal, utensils used for eating, and more. They can draw or cut and paste pictures from magazines to fit any of these categories. After drawing, have each student list the items on the plate if there is space for writing or on the back of the page. Students can also use the reproducible to draw a favorite food before or after they write directions for making it. Or, they can write any of these lists right on the plate instead of drawing.

List Writing Activities

- At the beginning of the first day of school, have students list things they think might happen on that day. At the end of the day, let them highlight all of the things from their lists that occurred. (Do not ask students to cross out anything that did not happen since that looks like they got it wrong, and who wants to be wrong on the first day of school?) Let volunteers share their lists aloud.

- Host a class social to break the ice. On the first day of school, serve snacks and drinks while students walk around the room and make lists of their classmates' names. When students are seated again, let a student name a fellow classmate, have that student name another classmate, and so on. Record the names on the board until all students are listed.

- Get to know students' ambitions and talents. Invite each student to list five things she wants to learn during the school year. Next, ask her to list five things she is great at doing. These lists will help you personalize each student's classroom experience. For example, if you have a student who writes that she wants to learn about tornadoes, you can incorporate a lesson or two into a preexisting weather unit. If you have a student who is good at kickball, schedule a few games during recess. Each student will get a chance to achieve a couple of goals and an opportunity to shine.

- Have students make lists of things that it takes to be a great teacher. Make your own list. During class writing time, compile all answers. Post the five that are most frequently mentioned.

- Repeat the above assignment but list things that make a great student. Post the compiled student list next to the teacher list.

- Combine lists with lunching. Encourage each student to make a list of what he has in his lunch box. Then, have each student make a list of what he wishes he had in his lunch box. (This would be a great list to make on the **Write-On Plate** reproducible.)

- Use the old standard of letting students help you brainstorm a list of class rules as you write them on the board or overhead. Have students copy the final list in their journals. Consider asking students to sign their lists stating that they will follow the rules. Post the rules in the classroom.

- Turn a class birthday into a writing assignment. On the first student birthday, let the class make wish lists of what they want to receive for their own birthdays.

- If you are able to offer television or video viewing as a special treat, let each student list her three favorite shows or films. Use the complied lists as a guide for what to show in class during treat time.

- Do not forget that lists provide instant feedback. In the middle of the school year, ask each student to make a list of five things he likes about school and then list five things he wishes were different about school. These lists will give you insight into what is going well and what is not. It will also help you identify classmates who may be struggling to get along. A good time to assign this list is a week or two before parent-teacher conferences.

- As a reward for their hard work in reading, take students to the media center for a title find. Have each student look around the room and copy the titles of five or six books that she would like to read. (This would be a great list to make on the **Decorative Blank List** or **Journal Page** reproducible.) Remind students to bring their lists with them on library trips and check out those titles.

- Ask students: If they could eat in class, what five foods would they like to have? Have them write a list on the **Write-On Plate** reproducible. Tally the results and bring in the top three or four foods for students to enjoy during the next writing period. *(Note: Check school guidelines and be aware of student allergies.)* Remind them that this is a tangible reward for their writing.

Utilitarian Writing Activities

- Remember those sweet notes you got from little friends that said, "Do you like me? Check *yes* or *no*." Let students make their own surveys to share with the class that are based on checking boxes. Suggest "favorite things" topics like *dogs* or *ice cream flavors* but let students come up with their own ideas as much as possible. Encourage each student to make a survey about likes and dislikes and finish the form by drawing boxes to check. Screen the surveys beforehand for legibility and appropriate content; then, copy and distribute them as you would any other assignment. You may want to assign the **Camp Windy Woods Application** first as a model for making this type of list.

- If your school has a fund-raiser with order forms, such as a cookie sale, book sale, or wrapping paper sale, gather several copies of the fund-raiser catalog and place them in a box in a center. Copy the order forms and place the copies in the box along with pencils. When students visit the center, let them practice filling out the order forms.

- Ask parents to collect comment cards when they eat at restaurants or stay in hotels. Place copies of those cards in a center. Let students pretend they have eaten out or taken a vacation and then fill out a comment card for each.

- Show students how to fill out an envelope properly. Pass out real envelopes to the class. Students can practice filling out their own addresses as the return address and then either make up addresses or use real ones for the recipients' addresses.

Cross-Curricular Utilitarian Assignments

- **Language Arts:** Have students write a different kind of "book report." Create a simple form to let students report book damage. On a half sheet of paper, write the following, including an answer line after each: *Book Title, Book Author, Kind of Damage, Page Number Where Damage Was Found*. Store the forms in your classroom library and encourage students to fill out a report when they find a book with torn or missing pages, marks, or dirt.

- **Math:** If it is cookie-sale time for any local school or organization, copy a cookie order form. Place the copies in a center and allow a few students at a time an opportunity to read the cookie descriptions, mark the forms, count their boxes, and add up their totals.

- **Social Studies:** Do calendar work with students by giving them a blank calendar page at the beginning of each month. Have students fill in the names of the days and month, the dates, and any holidays or special observances that fall during that month.

- **Science:** Warning and instructional posters are a good source for utilitarian writing activities. Let students make posters with instructions to follow during a weather emergency. Use the severe weather that is most common in your area as the topic and inform students about classroom and school procedures so that they can make the posters accurate.

- **Health:** Have each student keep a log about her physical activity for a few days.

Evaluation Ideas

Again, since your writing program is just beginning, it is better to respond than to grade at this point. If, however, you are using these activities with a preexisting curriculum that calls for evaluation, create a rubric that includes details like accuracy (such as spelling the days and months correctly on the calendar) and completion of work.

Journals

Journal writing is often treated as a diary session for students, but for these assignments, you should forewarn students that you will collect their journals periodically. Making journal writing more focused is best for younger students since many of them are too young to generate a lot of text. Having students write in journals is a good idea. The benefits include the following: they can take their journals outside of the classroom, they can revisit old entries for writing ideas, and they can see how elements of their writing—such as the length of their written pieces, their handwriting skill, and the subjects about which they choose to write—have changed.

Special Tips for Journals

- If you decide to use journals, let students decorate the covers as their first writing assignment. Provide markers, stickers, and other art supplies to make it a fun project. You may wish to avoid glitter, since the journals will be handled often and the glitter will continually rub off.

- Give each student a notebook with a pocket in which to store loose assignments. Or, provide pocket folders in which students can store both their journals and loose papers. Some students may need to refer to a handwriting chart when writing, so have them store that tool in a pocket.

- Periodically clean out journals and folders by removing torn pages and loose papers that are no longer needed. Store published writing in a portfolio that does not travel with students. You may not want to send writing home since students can use their older writing as brainstorming to inspire newer pieces. They can also reuse older writing when you teach revision and publishing, so it is good to have it handy.

- Do not hesitate to let students draw in their journals. Some students find drawing easier and more engaging, and when you add a writing element to the drawing assignment, it helps them learn to associate a difficult task with one they enjoy.

Journals Reproducibles

- Use the **Journal Page** reproducible (page 20) for journal-type assignments you want students to turn in. If you decide not to use notebooks, make multiple copies of the page and then staple them together to make booklets.

- Provide copies of the **My Journal Page** reproducibles (pages 23 and 24) for any writing assignment to which you want to add a special element. Students can use these pages when recopying finished pieces for publishing.

Journal Writing Activities

Although these activities are specifically designed for journals, almost any assignment in this book can be written in a journal. If students are not able to write, let them draw or dictate their responses.

- On the first day of school, ask students to write or draw about what they hope will happen this year in school. When you collect the journals and read these entries, make a journal entry of your own that notes how you can try to address students' individual wishes.

- Get to know your students through journals. Have them write about a few things in which they excel and some things they would like to do better. To add an art element, have them draw pictures of themselves doing something they are good at. To put students at ease, write this journal entry yourself and share it aloud.

- Use journals to let students write about problems that crop up in the classroom. If there is a conflict between two students, have them write and/or draw about the problem but insist they spend more time focusing on what each of them would like to happen than on describing the conflict.

- Use a journal entry to get student feedback about possible field trips. Give them parameters, such as inviting them to choose between a few possibilities or allow them to brainstorm a list of ideas and then pick one to write about. You may get some very responses this way!

- If students seem to be progressing into thinking of journal writing ideas on their own, let them keep lists of writing ideas in the backs of their journals. Periodically, have them choose their own topics and write about them. For students who struggle with open-ended assignments, be available to help them choose topics and find reasons for their choices so that their writing is still purposeful.

Cross-Curricular Journal Assignments

- **Language Arts:** At the beginning of the year, use journals to assess where students are with their writing skills. Ask each student to write a few sentences about the best books he has ever read and draw a picture of the book cover. You will be able to see what kinds of books students are reading as you see how well they are currently writing. Have students save this writing assignment because you can have them revise the reports when their writing skills have improved, and you can also let them see if the books they chose as their favorites have changed later in the school year.

- **Math:** Letting students make up their own story problems is a popular way to determine whether they have grasped the last concept you taught. After they write the problems, check that the problems work and then post them in the room. Let students solve the posted problems.

- **Social Studies:** Use this activity at different times of the year depending on the holidays that students observe. Instruct each student to draw a picture of a favorite holiday tradition. Next, have her write five things her family does on that holiday.

- **Science:** The simplest way to incorporate journals into science lessons is to let students use their journals to record observations as they conduct investigations or learn new science concepts.

Evaluation Ideas

- One simple way to grade journal writing is to keep a list of assignments and then count to see if all are included.

- Once you set up the rubric, let each student choose the journal entry he wants you to evaluate.

- Because journals are informal, it is easy to jot down quick comments. Choose your words carefully so that students are comfortable with writing in their journals and are still learning.

Decorative Blank List

Name

Name

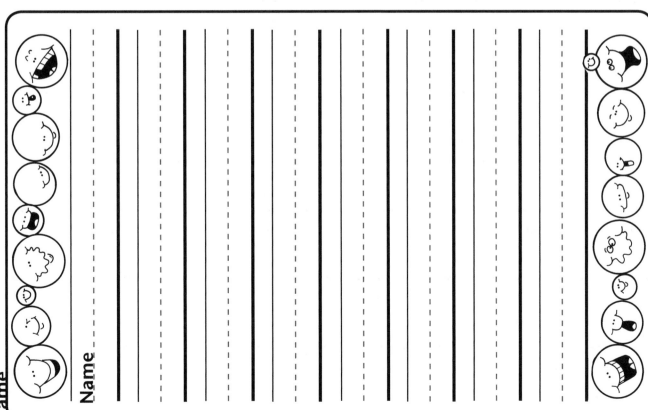

Name

Name

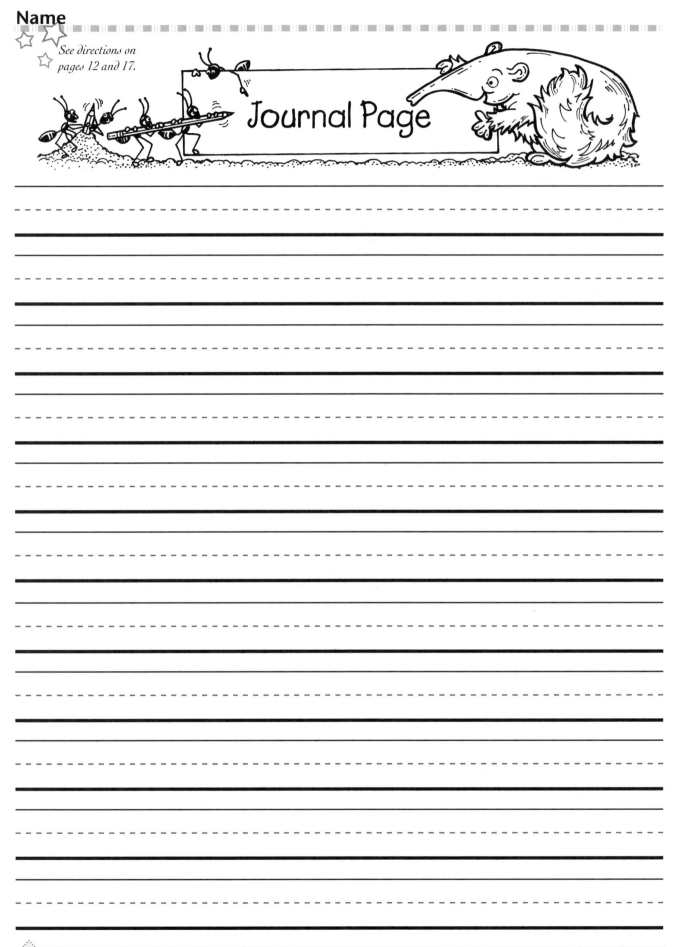

Name _____

See directions on pages 12 and 17.

Journal Page

 KE-804078 © Key Education • *Make Writing Exciting!*

See directions on page 12.

ABC Journal of

Gg

Hh

Ii

Jj

Kk

Ll

Aa

Bb

Cc

Dd

Ee

Ff

See directions on page 12.

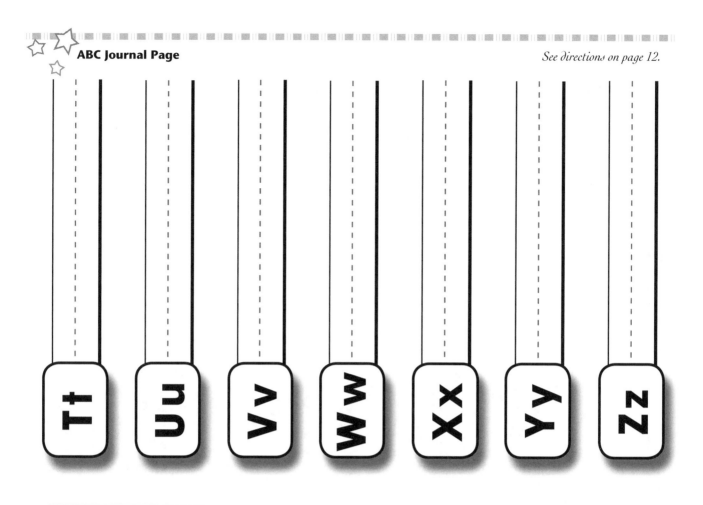

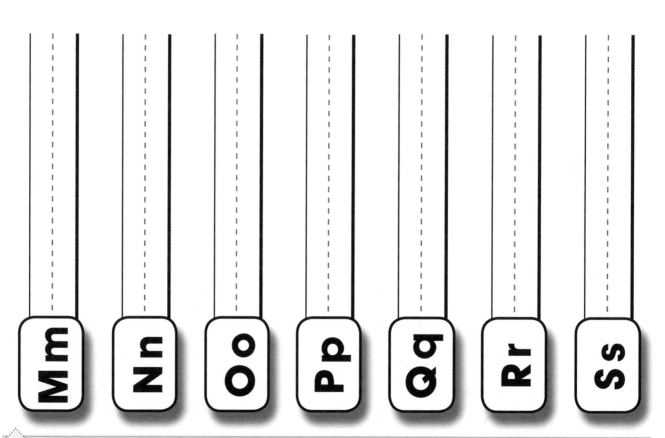

See directions on page 17.

My Journal Page

See directions on page 17.

My Journal Page

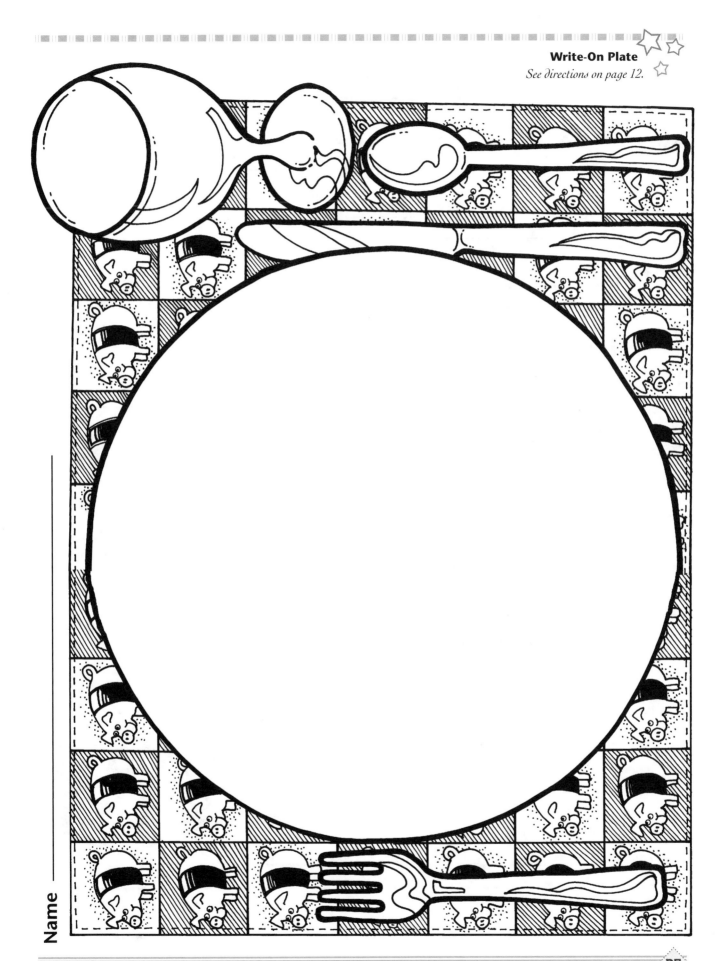

Name

✐➤ Fill in the blanks to ask a friend to come to a theme party.

You're invited . . .

_____

Please come to my _____ party.

Time: _____

Date: _____

RSVP: _____

Place: _____

(Your name)

✫ ✫
✫ ## Comment Card   _____

✐➤ Pretend you have just been to a restaurant, hotel, park or other place. Did you like the place? Would you go back? Fill in the blanks. Write two sentences on the back of this paper to tell more about your visit.

_____

Tell us about your visit at _____

Did you enjoy the visit? _____

Was the area clean? _____

Was the _____ good? _____

_____

Comments: _____

Camp Windy Woods
Application

✏️➤ It is time for summer camp! Fill in the blanks to help the counselors match you with good cabinmates.

Your full
name: _____

Your friends | Your birth
call you: _____ | date: ___ / ___ / ___

Your
address: _____

✏️➤ Tell us a little bit about yourself!

The kind of friend
I like is one who . . . _____

The kind of counselor
I like is one who . . . _____

✏️➤ Check **five** things you would like to do at camp.
Draw an **X** on **two** things you would NOT like to do.

☐ arts and crafts   ☐ drama   ☐ softball

☐ canoeing   ☐ hiking   ☐ swimming

☐ climbing   ☐ horseback riding   ☐ table tennis

☐ clowning   ☐ kickball   ☐ tumbling

☐ dancing   ☐ rocketry   ☐ woodworking

☐ diving   ☐ soccer   ☐ writing

✏️➤ On the back of this paper, tell us about what you hope will happen at camp this summer.

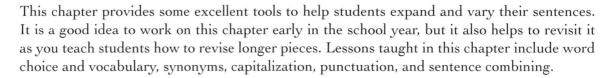

Superb Sentences

This chapter provides some excellent tools to help students expand and vary their sentences. It is a good idea to work on this chapter early in the school year, but it also helps to revisit it as you teach students how to revise longer pieces. Lessons taught in this chapter include word choice and vocabulary, synonyms, capitalization, punctuation, and sentence combining.

Special Tips for Sentences

- Teaching punctuation concepts along with sentence construction gives students a jump on becoming editors of their own and others' work.

- Word choice exercises work well when included with sentence instruction because sentences are compact and easy to play with. Searching for the best word will be more automatic if it is practiced early on.

- As students work on sentences, also take the opportunity to teach the standards of grammar and spelling that writers must adhere to so that their papers are readable. It is easier to start focusing on these with shorter writing exercises.

- For many young writers, even short, simple sentences will be hard work for a while. Be patient and offer lots of practice and praise.

Sentence Reproducibles

- The **Choosing Better Words** reproducible (page 32) helps students learn to replace some commonly overused or "tired" words with more descriptive ones. Introduce the new vocabulary words to the class. Have students work with partners and use the words listed on the right in sentences before they complete the reproducibles.

- The **Banking Some Words** reproducible (page 33) is a programmable vocabulary page that helps students work on sentences for any subject area. On a blank copy of the page, fill in the coins with words you would like students to use in a writing assignment. As a student incorporates one of the featured words in her writing, she may cut out and glue that coin on the bank.

- Have students complete the **Describe It!** reproducibles (pages 34 and 35) to practice writing sentences. By scaffolding the skills, students move towards generating their own sentences for open-ended subjects.

- The **Writing Interesting Sentences** reproducibles (pages 36–39) incorporate the six question words (*when, where, who, what, how,* and *why*) to guide students in expanding sentences. To use this activity with other sentences, cover the sentences on the reproducibles, write your own, and copy the page for students. Add a fun element by asking each student to write one of his new sentences on the back of the page and then illustrate it. (The **Planning Your Story** reproducible on page 123 also features the question words.)

- Use the **Missing Capital Letters** reproducibles (pages 40 and 41) to help students learn which words are traditionally capitalized. Read the directions with students and go over the different types of words that need capitalization (names, the pronoun *I,* specific places, initial words in sentences, etc.). To scaffold these skills, introduce one type of capitalization at a time and then review by completing Parts A–D in increments.

- The **Please Punctuate** reproducible (page 42) is a simple exercise in adding correct punctuation. Review the different types of ending punctuation before assigning Part A or B.

- The **You Be the Editor!** reproducibles (pages 43 and 44) offer more practice on capitalization and ending punctuation. If students are feeling overwhelmed by the task, edit one or two sentences at a time or have them first focus on filling in the missing ending punctuation. These exercises are a great review for Chapter 11: Convening with Conventions.

- Let students practice inserting commas by completing the reproducibles **Commas Needed** (page 45) and **Come On, Commas!** (page 46). Review comma usage before assigning the reproducibles. On page 45, Part A focuses on the need for commas to separate names in a series. Part B addresses the use of commas to separate distinct thoughts (between two independent clauses or between a dependent clause and an independent clause) in sentences. On page 46, students apply both of these skills.

- Students can complete the reproducibles **Prepositions on the Page** (page 47) and **Add a Prepositional Phrase** (page 48) to learn what prepositions are and how they can be used to expand sentences. Many students in this age group naturally use prepositional phrases in their speech. They do not need to recognize the word *preposition* and be able to list many examples. However, point out how easy it is to use prepositional phrases in their writing.

- The **Sentence Combo** reproducibles (pages 49 and 50) demonstrate how to combine short, choppy sentences to make longer, more interesting sentences. When introducing this skill, first have students make sentences that have compound subjects or predicates before moving on to other types of sentence combinations. Also, point out that not all sentences need to be long; a variety of sentence lengths also works well.

- Consider having students learn the symbols on the **Proofreaders' Marks** reproducible (page 140). They will be able to use some of the marks with the activities in this chapter.

- Assess students' sentence writing abilities by having them write 10 interesting sentences about a topic of their choice. When you collect the papers, you will immediately be able to tell who needs help with particular skills.

- Have an overused-word brainstorming session. On the board, make a list of overused words such as *fun*, *pretty*, and *happy*. Call them "tired" words. Have the class call out synonyms as you write them in a different color around the tired words. Next, instruct students to write sentences using each synonym.

- Let each student write a short sentence that contains an overused word of her choice. Ask students to pass their papers to classmates. Have each student write a synonym for the overused word on his classmate's paper. Trade papers several more times until each student has a list of four or five synonyms on his paper. Let students record the overused words and their synonyms in their journals to create their own thesauruses.

- This fill-in-the-blank activity works for many different parts of speech. Have each student copy these sentences on a piece of paper: *That was the _____ meal I have ever eaten* and *This is the _____ day of my life!* Challenge each student to come up with five words to fill in the blank for each sentence, but they cannot use *best* or *worst*. Let students share their funniest choices. Examples of other sentences might include *That smells _____!* (cannot use *good* or *bad*) and *The car _____ down the street* (cannot use *drove*).

- Demonstrate how a sentence changes with punctuation. On the board, write the sentence *Stop the car* three times without any ending punctuation. Let a student punctuate the first copy of the sentence and then include a sentence that goes with that punctuation. For example, the first pair of sentences might say *Stop the car! There's a cat in the road!* The second one might say *Stop the car. My house is right here.* The last sentence could say *Stop the car? But, we aren't there yet!* Provide students with a few sentences to work on independently, such as *Jump off the steps, Liam got sick yesterday,* and *Close the door.*

- Use plastic eggs to teach capitalization. On small pieces of paper, write a selection of words in lowercase letters. Some of them should be words that are always capitalized, like titles, days of the week, months of the year, I, classmates' names, the name of your school, etc. The remaining words should be improper nouns. Put each prepared piece of paper in a plastic egg. Make enough eggs to have two for each student. Hide the eggs around the room. Instruct each student to find two eggs, open them, look at the words, and decide whether they should be capitalized. Let students turn in their words and tell you which, if any, should be capitalized. Hide the eggs every day for several days until students recognize the capitalized words easily. Wrap up the activity by filling the plastic eggs with small treats to reward students' work and have them find those hidden eggs.

- Write some statements, questions, and exclamations on sentence strips. Leave off the ending punctuation. Create one strip for each student and one for yourself. Next, draw a large period on one index card, an exclamation point on another card, and a question mark on a third. Give these cards to a chosen student. Distribute the sentence strips to all students. Stand at the front of the room and hold up your sentence strip as you read the sentence. Have the student with the punctuation cards come to the front of the room and hold the appropriate punctuation mark at the end of your sentence strip. (There may be more than one right answer.) Next, let that student hold up his sentence, read it, and choose a classmate to hold up the appropriate punctuation card. Continue until all students have held up their sentence strips and a punctuation card.

- Add an art element to sentence combining. Have each student draw a self-portrait and then write descriptive sentences about herself based on the portrait: *My hair is dark blond. My eyes are blue. My hair is long. I am tall. I do not have bangs. My teeth are straight.* Tell students to combine their sentences so that there are fewer, longer sentences. For example, combine the sentences above to say: *My dark blond hair is long, and I don't wear bangs. I am taller than most kids in the class. I have straight teeth and blue eyes.*

- Do a sentence expander exercise with you as the subject. Write *The teacher* on the board and let students add verbs, prepositional phrases, adjectives, and clauses to expand it. You may want to recruit a teaching assistant to add to the sentence as you act out students' additions.

Cross-Curricular Sentence Assignments

- **Language Arts:** Copy a different page from an easy reader for each student. Let each student choose a sentence to rearrange. Have the student copy the old sentence and his new version on a piece of paper. If you have time, read the book aloud to the class, inserting each new sentence in place of an old one.

- **Math:** Help students study addition as well as sentence making. Write a simple sentence on the board, such as *Two plus two equals four*. Ask students how many different ways they could write this math problem, such as *Add two to two and you get four*, *Add two plus two more and the total will be four*, and so on. Write all correct answers on the board. Repeat this exercise with other addition and subtraction facts.

- **Social Studies:** If students are learning new social studies vocabulary, produce a word bank on chart paper and have students create interesting sentences with those words.

- **Science:** If the class is studying physical properties, have students write their observations in complete sentences. For example, if students are describing ice and what happens when it melts, they could write: *The ice is cold and wet. It is slippery when I pick it up. It makes my fingers hurt if I hold it for too long.*

- **Art:** Let students write a running commentary of sentences as you complete a piece of artwork. Start by drawing a few lines on the board and let each student write a sentence describing what you drew. As you add to the drawing, pause to allow time for students to keep writing. Continue to do this until the drawing is finished. Then, ask volunteers to read back their play-by-play descriptions.

Evaluation Ideas

As you start to teach about writing good sentences, respond only to one element or skill at first: word choice, capitalization, punctuation, sentence expansion or sentence combining. (Identifying prepositional phrases when including them in the sentences comes later.) Add new skills as students master the previous ones. Post a list of skills that students have already covered. Update the list with each newly acquired skill to emphasize how much students are learning.

Choosing Better Words

A

Look at the words on the left. Draw a line from each word to two more interesting words. On the back of this paper, write two sentences using some interesting words.

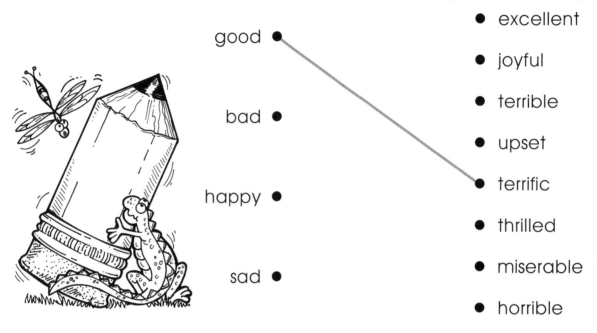

good ●   ● excellent
                  ● joyful
bad ●   ● terrible
                  ● upset
happy ●   ● terrific
                  ● thrilled
                  ● miserable
sad ●   ● horrible

Choosing Better Words

B

Look at the words on the left. Draw a line from each word to two more interesting words. On the back of this paper, write two sentences using some interesting words.

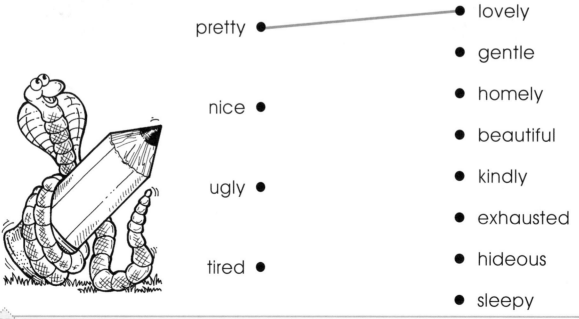

pretty ●   ● lovely
                  ● gentle
                  ● homely
nice ●   ● beautiful
                  ● kindly
ugly ●   ● exhausted
                  ● hideous
tired ●   ● sleepy

Banking Some Words

Make interesting sentences. As you use each word in your writing, cut out and glue that coin on the bank.

Describe It!

A

Read the sentences. Add words that describe. Then, rewrite the sentences.

1. The dog barked.

   The little white dog barked.

2. The bird chirped.

   _____

3. Look at the car!

   _____

4. He held the ball.

   _____

Describe It!

B

Read the sentences. Add words that describe. Then, rewrite the sentences.

1. I like my bike.

   _____

2. My dad drives the truck.

   _____

3. The girl looks at the house.

   _____

4. The man runs to the store.

   _____

Describe It! ⭐ C

Make sentences. Include words that describe. Write the sentences on the lines.

1. My puppy

My brown puppy licked my face.

2. The rabbit

3. My toys

4. Her kitten

Describe It! ⭐ D

Make sentences. Include words that describe. Write the sentences on the lines.

1. The lion

2. My mom

3. The boys

4. Some trucks

Writing Interesting Sentences

 A

✏️ Read the directions. Think about the *W* or *H* word (*when, where, who, what, why,* or *how*). Then, read the sentence in dark type. Rewrite that sentence to give more information. The first one is done for you.

1. Rewrite the sentence. Tell *when* the party happened.

I went to Lea's birthday party.

I went to Lea's birthday party last Saturday.

2. Rewrite the sentence. Tell *where* the party was held.

I was excited to go to the party.

_____

_____

3. Rewrite the sentence. Tell *who* was at the party.

I saw my friends when I got there.

_____

_____

Writing Sentences (Cont.)

A

4. Rewrite the sentence. Tell *what* was inside the box.

I carried in a large box for Lea.

_____

- -

_____

- -

_____

5. Rewrite the sentence. Tell *how* the box was wrapped.

I wrapped the box myself.

_____

- -

_____

- -

_____

- -

_____

6. Rewrite the sentence. Tell *why* the writer likes Lea.

I like Lea.

_____

- -

_____

- -

_____

Name _____

Writing Interesting Sentences **B**

✏️ Read the directions. Think about the *W* or *H* word (*when, where, who, what, why,* or *how*). Then, read the sentence in dark type. Rewrite that sentence to give more information.

I. Rewrite the sentence. Tell *when* the writer left.

I left for Big Woods Camp.

_____

- -

_____

2. Rewrite the sentence. Tell *where* the camp is located.

Dad drove me to the camp.

_____

- -

_____

- -

_____

3. Rewrite the sentence. Tell *who* was at the camp.

When I got there, I saw my friends.

_____

- -

_____

- -

_____

4. Rewrite the sentence. Tell *what* they did at the camp.

We did many things.

_____

- -

_____

_____

- -

_____

_____

- -

_____

5. Rewrite the sentence. Tell *how* and *when* the writer got home.

I went home.

_____

- -

_____

_____

- -

_____

6. Rewrite the sentence. Tell *why* the writer likes the camp.

I like the camp.

_____

- -

_____

_____

- -

_____

Missing Capital Letters   A

Read the sentences. Look for the pronoun *I* and the names of people. Look for the first word in each sentence. Cross out the small letters that are wrong. Write capital letters above them. Two words are done for you.

1. M
   ~~m~~om wants me to help her make dinner.

   A
   ~~a~~fter the meal, i am running to bert's house.

2. this evening, we are playing soccer with austin, john, and bella.

   i hope sam, megan, and nate can also play with us.

3. i know that dad will help set up the field.

4. we are excited about playing two games with the smith family.

Missing Capital Letters   B

Read the sentences. Look for the pronoun *I* and names of people and specific places, Also look for the first word in each sentence. Cross out the small letters that are wrong. Write capital letters above them.

1. today, we can ride our bikes down big pond road.

   we will buy food for my dog at al's pet food supply.

2. in sunnyville, i like to ride my bike down main street.

3. will you help david give the dogs a bath?

4. let's take the dogs to high hills park to run.

   mark, chen, and sora will meet us there.

Missing Capital Letters

Read the sentences. Look for the pronoun *I* and the names of people and specific places. Look for the first word in each sentence. Cross out the small letters that are wrong. Write capital letters above them.

1. my friend ava has three brothers.

her brothers' names are lance, ty, and colin.

2. wait for jorge and his sister marta to arrive.

marta says that you and i can go with her to the mall.

3. jenny likes to play golf. Her favorite golf course is spring hills.

4. we went to wiggle worm bait shop before dad took us fishing.

jen caught an old boot and i caught three fish!

- -

 Name

Missing Capital Letters

Read the sentences. Find the missing capital letters. Cross out the small letters that are wrong. Write capital letters above them.

1. on sunday, we will have a big dinner at grandma's.

grandma makes chicken pie in the winter.

2. tywan's birthday is on january fifth.

he wants a scooter.

3. i like to read books. may i go to walker library on saturday?

4. my dog's name is thomas and my cat's name is percy.

i also have a bird named henry.

Please Punctuate **A**

Read the sentences. Add a period or question mark to each one.

1. Can you come over for dinner   We are having tacos

2. My favorite food is pizza   What foods do you like

3. Would you like a snack   I can make it

4. Please melt the cheese

I will put the chips on a dish

5. Let's find the deck of cards

Which card game would you like to play

Please Punctuate **B**

Read the sentences. Add a period, question mark, or exclamation point to each one.

1. Do not run into the street   I will get the ball for you

2. Tomorrow is Hat Day at school   I will wear my baseball cap

3. Did you know that Cam got chicken pox

He feels better now

4. Max just hit a home run   He is a good hitter

5. Surprise, Ally   We are happy to see you

You Be the Editor!

A

Fix the sentences. Read the story and find the errors. Fill in the missing capital letters and punctuation. Use tally marks to keep track of the errors you find.

What's Needed	Tally Marks
12 capital letters	
3 periods	
2 question marks	
1 exclamation point	

Can you guess what i did this summer My Aunt liz and Uncle Jon own a camp. It is on Lake james   It is called Camp Canyonlands.   Last august, I was finally old enough to go   I stayed in a cabin with five other boys.   Their names were Ian, Caleb, John, Andre, and Evan.   My bunk was over Ian's bunk.   It was next to John's bunk.   The first night, we all wrote letters.   I wrote to my sister katie.   The other boys were a little homesick.   My aunt and uncle came to see me, so I was not sad.   They brought us cookies.   in the morning, Ian helped me make my bed.   I helped john make his bed.   we all sat together at breakfast. We played basketball.   We went swimming in lake james.   After lunch, we rode horses.   My horse was named snowball.   What color do you think she was   She was a black horse!   We had a campfire at dinner. we toasted hot dogs and marshmallows.   We were very tired and went to sleep fast   My first day of camp was great

Name

You Be the Editor!

B

Fix the sentences. Read the story and find the errors. Fill in the missing capital letters and punctuation. Use tally marks to keep track of the errors you find.

What's Needed	Tally Marks
10 capital letters	
6 periods	
2 question marks	
2 exclamation points	

I go to midlands School. Today, I am staying home It is a snow day. it is the sixth snow day we have had in january.   It is freezing outside! mom says we are going to make ice skaters today.   first, she put a pan of water in the freezer   Next, she gave me a clothespin.   I drew eyes and a face on it   I named my skater Lily   Mom filled a paper cup with water.   We put the clothespin in the cup.   Mom put it in the freezer when we took it out later, can you guess what happened   It froze

I peeled off the cup. There was a block of ice around the clothespin. mom took out the pan of ice.   Now, my skater lily can slide across her very own ice rink.   I can't wait to show my friend Nora.   mom said I can help nora make her own skater   Then, we can play together.   Do you think there will be a snow day tomorrow   I hope so

Name _____

Commas Needed
A

 The commas are missing. They are needed to separate the names of three or more things or people in a series. Add commas to each sentence.

1. I looked for my bat baseball and glove.

2. Mom drove Makayla Mitch and me to the ball field.

3. My team wore red white and black shirts.

4. We ate popcorn peanuts and watermelon after the game.

5. There are ball games on Tuesday Thursday and Saturday.

- -

Name _____

Commas Needed
B

 A comma is used to separate the first thought from the second in a sentence. Add commas to the sentences.

1. Before we left the house we had to put away our toys.

2. After driving to the park we ran from the car to the pool.

3. Everyone is ready to swim but I forgot my towel.

4. I left my towel in the car so I ran back to get it.

5. The sunshine is hot so my mom

is sitting in the shade.

Come On, Commas!

The commas are missing! Read each sentence out loud. Listen for places where you stop to take a breath. Add commas to the sentences in the places where you pause.

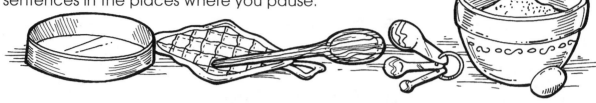

1. On my friend Tom's birthday I was making a cake.

2. I went to the store to buy butter eggs and milk.

3. After making the cake I made the icing.

4. Tom Drew and Beth were waiting for me at the party.

5. It was time for me to leave so I got a box to put the cake in.

6. Since I needed to hurry I rushed out the door.

7. I tripped on the step fell down and dropped the box!

8. When the box fell open I saw that it was empty.

9. I had put in the cake plate but I forgot to put in the cake.

10. When I got to the party I was late. Everyone liked my cake!

Prepositions on the Page

Some words tell you where things are. A good way to find these words is to fill in the blank in this sentence.

The airplane flew _____ the cloud.

✎ Circle all of the words that could be used to fill in the blank above.

fast	under	happy	with
over	two	near	den
full	square	inside	beside
around	by	red	time
plan	book	to	at

✎ Read the sentence starters. Draw a line to finish each one.

1. The skunk sprayed my dog   next to mine.

2. My friend parked her scooter   in the face.

3. Our team played soccer   over the fence.

4. We had to put the blocks   on the field.

5. The horse jumped   up the ladder.

6. I climbed   in the bin.

Add a Prepositional Phrase

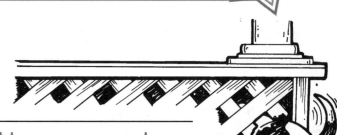

Complete each sentence with a phrase that tells where. End each sentence with a period. The first one has been done for you.

1. The dog ran _under the porch._

2. The girl jumped _____

3. I like to play _____

4. My teacher lives _____

5. The birds built their nest _____

6. The cat walked _____

7. The boy sprinted _____

8. The tiger leaped _____

9. The girls sat _____

Sentence Combo

 Combine these sentences. You can add or change words if you need to. You can also change punctuation. Every other sentence has been done for you.

1. Ron got dressed. He went to school.

| and then |

Ron got dressed and then went to school.

Katie ate lunch. She went outside.

- -

2. Ginny likes cake. Ginny likes pie.

| and |

Ginny likes cake and pie.

Dean plays the piano. Dean plays the drums.

- -

3. Padma made lunch. Padma did not make dinner.

| but |

Padma made lunch but did not make dinner.

Fred took a bath. Fred did not brush his teeth.

- -

Sentence Combo

✏️ Combine these sentences. You can add or change words if you need to.
You can also change punctuation. Every other sentence has been done for you.

1. Sarah wants to fly her kite. There is no wind.

but

Sarah wants to fly her kite, but there is no wind.

I want to play outside. It is raining.

_____

- -

_____

2. We ran around the track. My coach ran around the track.

with

We ran around the track with my coach.

The geese swam in the pond. The goslings swam in the pond.

_____

- -

_____

- -

3. Rosa baked the cupcakes. She frosted them.

and then

Rosa baked the cupcakes and then frosted them.

Jamel ran to the park. He slid down the slide.

_____

- -

_____

- -

Topic Talk

As students work on longer writing assignments, they will need to learn brainstorming and prewriting and then expanding and narrowing topics. First, it is important that students understand they are brainstorming and prewriting to look for topics and main ideas. Students should learn that every piece of writing has a topic/main idea and that brainstorming will help them find topics to guide their writing. This knowledge makes brainstorming more relevant and focused.

Special Tips for Topics

- Gauge whether students are ready to differentiate between a topic (my dog) and a main idea (Training my dog was hard work). Not every writing program or teacher makes this distinction, but you will need to know which one you mean when you teach this terminology. Your school's curriculum may dictate the term as well as its meaning, so check there first.

- To start a discussion about topics and main ideas, use pictures and then paragraphs from textbooks and children's books. Paragraphs are more straightforward than longer pieces of writing. Their topics are easier for students to identify.

- Get students into the habit of picking out the topics/main ideas in their own writing. Ask students to take turns reading their first drafts aloud and then let classmates say what they think is the topic.

Topic Reproducibles

- The **Main Idea Pictures** reproducibles (pages 54 and 55) give students practice with finding the main idea in pictures, so it also gives them practice with picture prompts. Students should write what they think is the main idea under each picture.

- Use the **Topic Finders** reproducibles (pages 56 and 57 to help students find the topic or main idea in paragraphs. Have students circle each correct answer from the available choices. Otherwise, copy the paragraphs for the overhead, discuss the stories with the class, and have students work together to identify the topic sentences.

- The **Topic Match** reproducible (page 58) reinforces how the main idea and the details in a story are linked. Let students match the detail sentences to the correct main topics. Model this task for students before they do it on their own. As each student finishes, ask her to draw a picture that represents each group of sentences. For a companion activity, use the **Topic Sentence Match** reproducibles (pages 86 and 87) in Chapter 6: Paragraph Power.

Topic Activities

- If students are reading chapter books, choose a book with short chapters. (Students who are not reading chapter books can still do this exercise if you assign a short picture book that you have read in class.) Assign each small group one chapter. Let the students decide what they think is the main idea of their assigned chapter. Walk around to help any groups that are stuck. When all groups have finished, ask them to report to the class. List the main ideas in chronological order on the board and then read them back to students. Discuss how this list can become a good summary for the book. Good books for this exercise include the Frog and Toad series by Arnold Lobel (HarperCollins), the Ready, Freddy! series by Abby Klein (Blue Sky Press) and the Junie B. Jones series by Barbara Park (Random House Books for Young Readers).

- Ask each student to tell a short story about something he did over the summer. After a student finishes, invite classmates to raise their hands and state what the main idea of the student's story was. For example, explain that *What Matt did over the summer* is not the best answer for the main idea because it is not specific enough. The main idea has to be relevant to each student's specific story. *A trip to Disney World was the best part of Matt's summer* would make a much better main idea.

- Direct each student to fold over the top 2 in. (5 cm) of a piece of paper and then open it. Above the fold line, have each student write a different topic, such as *ice cream*. Below the fold line, each student should write details that are related to the chosen topic. For ice cream, those details might include *vanilla, chocolate, sprinkles, cold, creamy, nuts, spoon, bowl, cherries,* etc. Next, let students trade papers and try to guess each other's topic without peeking. Alternatively, ask students to reveal one detail from their lists at a time to the class to see which classmate guesses the topic first.

- Restating the main idea helps students think beyond copying what is on the page to writing sentences of their own. Give students a paragraph to read and direct them to identify the sentence that states the main idea. Have each student rewrite the sentence. For example, if the main idea of a paragraph is *Bike riding is a fun hobby, but be sure to wear a helmet to protect your head*, then the rewrite could say *Biking is fun, but you should always put on a helmet to make sure your head is protected*. This is a simple exercise that can be challenging for students. Be sure to offer guidance. After the rewrite is finished, direct students to compare the two sentences to determine if they contain the same information.

Cross-Curricular Topics Assignments

- **General:** Complete the restating the main idea activity as explained on the previous page with chapters from student textbooks. You will be reinforcing their learning as you also work on their writing skills.

- **General:** Modify the above activity. Instead of first reading the paragraphs in their textbooks, have students look at section titles. Ask them to predict what they think the sections will be about. Read the paragraphs and see whether their predictions were correct. Discuss the fact that some titles may be trying to catch readers' interest, and so the section titles may not reveal exactly what is in the text.

- **General:** Have students try to predict the main idea in textbook paragraphs by looking only at the pictures and captions. Again, discuss whether students were successful in identifying the main idea.

- **Language Arts:** Distribute copies of a book order flyer to the class. Have each child choose a book selection and predict the main idea of that book by looking at the picture of its cover. You should also do this exercise any time you introduce a new book to read aloud to students.

Evaluation Ideas

Evaluating the understanding of main idea is pretty straightforward. Students must know that they need to demonstrate comprehension of any text they are reading. If you want to add an oral element to evaluations, have them state the main idea of a story or paragraph in their own words. These are reading exercises, but if a student can identify a main idea in her reading, she should also be able to produce one in her writing.

Main Idea Pictures

 A

✏️ Look at each picture. Write the main idea under each picture.

1

_____

_____

_____

2

_____

_____

_____

Main Idea Pictures

Look at each picture. Write the main idea under each picture.

Topic Finders

 A

 Read each paragraph. Circle the main idea at the bottom.

Story A Mom and Dad were acting strangely. Mom did a lot of laundry in one day. Dad called Aunt Lauren and asked her to feed our dog. I did not know what was going on. I hoped nothing bad was happening. When I asked Dad, he told me not to worry. They made me go to bed very

early one night. When I woke up, I was in the car. I was still wearing pajamas! I asked where we were going. Mom said we were going to Disneyland! I was so excited that I could not fall back to sleep for the whole trip. It was a great surprise.

Mom and Dad   A surprise trip   Going to bed early

Story B

Huge storms can start over the ocean. These storms are called *hurricanes*. Some hurricanes move over land. They have strong winds and make lots of rain. Some hurricanes cause floods. When a big hurricane is near, people put boards over their windows. They leave their homes to find safe places to stay. They do not come home until the storm is over.

Hurricanes   Flooding   Big storm

Name

Topic Finders B

✏️ Read each paragraph. Circle the main idea at the bottom.

Story A   My brother and I wanted a pet. We cannot have a dog or cat. We both sneeze around animals with fur. Mom took us to the pet store to see other pets. We liked the fish tanks. The fish were very pretty swimming around inside. These were the pets that we  wanted. Mom helped us pick out a tank. We took it home and put clean, small rocks on the bottom. Then, we filled it with water. We added some plants and a pump that made bubbles in the back. We tested the water every day. When it was ready, Mom let us buy six fish. Mine were orange swordtails. My brother's fish were tiny. They were red and blue neons. Our fish like their new home. They swim around all day. We are happy with our new pets.

The pet store   Pet allergies   New pets

Story B

   I love Tuesdays! On Tuesdays, I visit my Nana's house. She always does fun things with me. We play marbles. She lets me type on her computer. We send e-mails to my dad at work. We go outside to pick flowers. She likes me to pick the little yellow ones because they are weeds. They do not smell good! The best part of the day is when we cook. She lets me make muffins. After we eat, we wash the dishes with lots of soap. I love my Nana very much.

Cooking   Tuesdays   Visiting Nana

Topic Match

✏️ Each main idea has **four** details. Draw a line from the box to each detail.

Topic A

Frogs are very interesting animals.

Topic B

I liked being the catcher at baseball practice.

Topic C

The pink pants my mom bought for me are very cool!

- My coach showed me how to pull off the mask and catch a foul ball.

- They grow legs and lose their tails.

- I had to go shopping for a new pair of pants.

- They are so loud when they croak at night!

- I like the stars sewn on the pockets.

- This was my first time behind home plate.

- Pink is my very favorite color.

- I threw a ball all the way to second base.

- The tadpoles look like tiny fish.

- I can wear them with my new pink tennis shoes.

- The adults catch bugs with their sticky tongues.

- The catcher's gear was heavy.

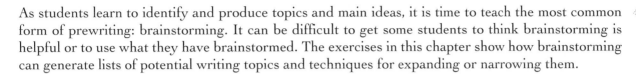

Prewriting with a Purpose

As students learn to identify and produce topics and main ideas, it is time to teach the most common form of prewriting: brainstorming. It can be difficult to get some students to think brainstorming is helpful or to use what they have brainstormed. The exercises in this chapter show how brainstorming can generate lists of potential writing topics and techniques for expanding or narrowing them.

Special Tips for Brainstorming and Other Prewriting

- All kinds of things count as prewriting: research, interviewing, illustrating, etc. It is not all about drawing webs. When students do any of these things, tell them that they could use the work as inspiration for future writing ideas.

- If students have produced lists, they have already had some practice with brainstorming. Revisit all of the early list-writing exercises in this book as sources of ideas for longer pieces.

- Students can get stuck on brainstorming because an assignment is too open-ended. Do some focused brainstorming to get them used to the process. For example, tell students they are going to write letters. Give them the audience for the letter and have them choose the topic. If you supply students with part of the picture and have them brainstorm what's missing, they will become more comfortable with the process and will soon be able to brainstorm all elements of the assignment.

Brainstorming and Other Prewriting Reproducibles

- Use the **Blank Journal Page** reproducible (page 20) to have students brainstorm lists of things they might like to write about. If students find that activity too open-ended, focus the assignment by having them list just funny stories they want to tell, or just people or nonfiction topics they want to write about.

- The **Regular Web** reproducible (page 63) is a spider-shaped illustration that students can use for simple brainstorming. To make the exercise more interactive as students write stories based on their webs, have them highlight the details when used.

- Kinesthetic learners will enjoy the cut-and-paste aspect of the **Cutout Web Organizer** reproducible (page 64). This reproducible should be used like a regular web at first. Direct students to write a main idea in the square box and then add details to the other boxes. Let them cut out the boxes and arrange them in the order that makes sense to tell about the topic. As a student incorporates each detail in his writing, he should glue it onto another sheet of paper that will be turned in with the written work. When you evaluate

papers, note which details students used. Talk with them about the decisions they made in their writing.

- The **Tornado Topic Organizer** reproducible (page 65) helps students narrow their topics. Place a copy of the organizer on the overhead. Note that it is shaped like a tornado. Write a very broad topic on the top line of the organizer. For example, you could write *dogs*. In the next space, write a narrowed topic, like *my dog*. Continue by writing *My dog digs*. In the bottom space, write *My dog dug up a snake and ate it*. Ask if students would be more interested in reading about this topic than about the topic *dogs*. Then, distribute the organizer and let students practice using it.

- The **Brick Wall Organizer** reproducible (page 66) is a cut-apart page that helps students put their ideas in order. Have students brainstorm events or details in a story by writing one item in each brick. Before students transition to writing, have them cut apart the bricks and arrange them in a column by gluing the pieces on a large piece of paper in the order they think the events should occur.

Brainstorming and Other Prewriting Activities

Most of these assignments are meant to teach brainstorming and do not contain instructions for turning the brainstorming into writing. However, you can use any of these to create actual writing assignments, either by pairing them with ideas in the Chapter 6: Paragraph Power and Chapter 7: Strong Stories or by adding your own ideas to them.

- Let students look back at their lists and other journal assignments and use a marker to circle the ideas they might want to use in the future. If you need a quick, easy writing assignment, let each student flip back through her journal to look for circled ideas and choose one to use as a topic for more brainstorming and then writing.

- Use students' listing skills as a scaffold—a basic skill on which they can build more writing. Have students generate lists of everything they need do during the week. Encourage them to list things that are slightly out of the ordinary like sports practices, tests, visits, etc. Then, tell students they have just brainstormed a list of writing topics. Invite students to imagine that they have to get all of the things done in one day. Help them write silly stories about what would happen. Would they need a flying car? Would they have to roll a piano onto the field during soccer practice? It would be a good idea to brainstorm a list and write your own story to share as an example.

- Do a class brainstorm about good writing ideas. Start with a few of your own that relate to things you are studying or doing in class. For example, if you are studying alligators, you might write *Alligators are good hunters.* Or, if you are getting ready to celebrate the 100th day, the topic could be *The 100th day is the best day of the school year.* After you brainstorm several good topics, write each one on a piece of chart paper. Display the papers around the room and invite students to walk around and add details to them. Read the lists aloud as a class and eliminate any off-

topic details. When students are ready to write longer papers, post the lists again and direct students to move their chairs to sit in front of the topics they want to write about. This will automatically create small groups for students to read and respond to each other's papers.

- Use "expert sticks" to create a crafty brainstorming assignment that allows each student to show off his expertise. Give each student a small stack of craft sticks and have him write one thing at which he is an expert on each stick. Model your own list so that students know they may include nonacademic things. For example, your list might consist of *teaching, making cookies, favorite music group: The Beatles, favorite author: J.K. Rowling,* and *taking care of the class hamster.* Next, have students turn their craft sticks face down, mix them up, and draw one. Give each student a sentence strip. Have him glue the chosen craft stick onto the left edge of the sentence strip and then brainstorm details on the rest of the strip. To save this for a future assignment, roll up each sentence strip and secure it with a paper clip on each side. Wrap a rubber band around the craft sticks to store them, as well. To complete the assignment, let each student write a draft explaining why he considers himself an expert on the chosen topic. Students should copy their final drafts on poster boards and then staple their sentence strips to the tops. Let them keep the bundles of craft sticks for future assignments.

- Make brainstorming more visual and concrete. Place a pile of construction paper in assorted colors, several pairs of scissors, and sheets of writing paper in a central location. Direct each student to cut out several different colored pieces of construction paper, explaining that every piece must be large enough for two words. To make "modern-art" mosaics, have students glue their small irregularly shaped pieces of construction paper onto sheets of writing paper to cover them completely. Set aside the papers to dry. Finally, explain to each student that she has to print a different writing idea on each construction-paper shape. When you have students use these papers later, assign a certain color. For example, if you select the color orange, students must write about a topic printed in one of their orange-colored pieces.

- Show students how to narrow topics. Let students brainstorm broad topics, such as *school*, *pets*, and *friends*, and then select one to narrow. For example, if students choose the broad topic *school*, you can direct them to list narrower topics, such as *the awesome new playground equipment*, *Pizza day is great*, *I won my event at field day*, *It takes too long for me to get ready for school in the morning*, etc. If a student suggests a topic that is still broad, such as the playground, ask, "What about the playground?" She should respond with a more specific topic. This will help produce precise writing ideas.

- Involve parents in a brainstorming homework assignment. Send home a journal or a notepad with each student and request the family to list the things that occur over the weekend. Ask them to keep in mind that one item on the list will be used for a writing assignment. Encourage parents and students to "think outside the box." Each list will contain events, such as family outings, but it could also contain mundane things that are gold mines for ideas. For example, most students could easily write about a weekend trip to Grandma's house, but it might be more interesting to write about helping their parents work in the backyard or how they fight with their siblings over who has to take out the garbage. Anything can become a writing topic!

- By this age, most students are allowed to watch television at home. Use T.V. as motivation for writing. Ask each student to write the name of his favorite television show at the top of a piece of paper and list reasons why he likes it, the characters, the plot of a recent episode he saw, etc. If you assign this activity as homework, students can complete it while they are watching their favorite shows.

- Add a visual element to any brainstorming session. After students finish brainstorming, have them draw pictures of what they brainstormed. Review each student's drawing and discuss which details from the list did not make it into the drawing and which details were added to the picture that were not recorded in the brainstorm list. Let students create pieces of writing inspired by the pictures.

- After students finish a web but before they write about it, demonstrate how to make simple outlines of the things they brainstormed. Use the **Brick Wall Organizer** reproducible or make a traditional outline. All students will see how to proceed in their writing without getting events out of order. Students with special needs may benefit from using an outline to help them create clear opening and closing statements.

Cross-Curricular Brainstorming and Other Prewriting Assignments

- **Language Arts:** Picture books are a great jumping-off point for brainstorming.

  - ▶ After reading *Kitten's First Full Moon* by Kevin Henkes (HarperCollins, 2004), have each student brainstorm details about a time when she was allowed to go outside at night. What did she see? What did it sound like and smell like? How was it different from being outside during the day?

  - ▶ Share *Cloudy with a Chance of Meatballs* by Judi Barrett (Aladdin, 1982). For an easy assignment, ask each student to brainstorm foods he would like to have fall from the sky for each meal. Have him list those foods and then make an outline for a story describing his day of meals from the sky.

  - ▶ Use *Harold and the Purple Crayon* by Crockett Johnson (HarperCollins, 1998) to inspire a writing and drawing assignment. Before students arrive for the day, cover the classroom walls with butcher paper. Place a purple crayon on each student's desk. When students arrive, share the book and then instruct them to get up and draw all over the paper. Turn on some music and let them draw for half an hour or as long as their interest holds. Afterwards, have them sit down, look at what they have drawn, and then brainstorm things they could write about. Let them use purple crayons to write, of course!

- **Math:** If students are tackling word problems, ask what subjects they think they would find interesting in math problems. Let students brainstorm lists of topics for good word problems and help them compose problems as they come up with topics.

- **Social Studies:** If you are teaching a lesson on a historical figure, brainstorm about that person's accomplishments with students. Add a research element by letting students read about the person before brainstorming. Explain to them that doing research can be a part of prewriting and brainstorming.

- **Science:** Have students brainstorm story ideas using whatever science concepts you are currently teaching. For example, if you are teaching the water cycle, let students brainstorm events in a story about a water molecule that goes through the water cycle. This is a complicated assignment that you will need to do as a class, but after evaluating the brainstorming your students have completed, you will be able to gauge their level of understanding of the scientific concept.

- **Health:** Take students outside to the playground and sit in a circle. Ask them to look around and think about other things they wish were on the playground. Brainstorm a list of cool playground additions as a class. During writing time, allow students to use the brainstormed list to write a descriptive paragraph of how they would like to improve their playground.

Evaluation Ideas

Brainstorming can be hard to evaluate because you are really assessing the student's creative processes. Some students may need to create elaborate brainstorms to come up with good writing ideas, while others may not need to brainstorm much at all and will find this step just extra work. When writing assignments evolve from brainstorming, you can give credit for this stage if it has been done, as well as whether the details listed in the brainstorm made it into the draft. (Have students complete the **Cutout Web** reproducible to help you evaluate their use of this strategy.)

Name _____

✏️ Write your topic on the spider's body. Draw a picture of it on the back of this paper. On each leg, write a detail about your chosen topic.

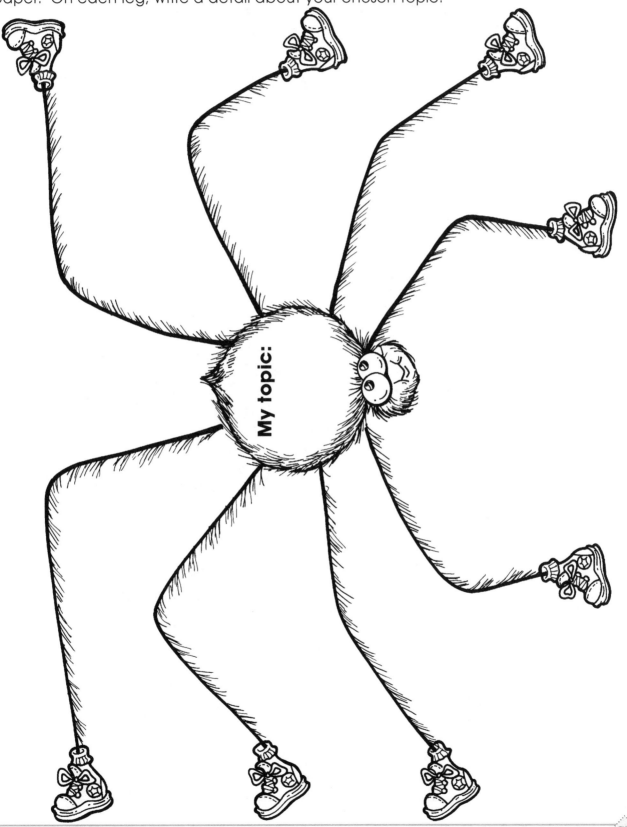

My topic:

Name _____

✏️➤ Write your topic in the square box. Write details in the smaller boxes Cut out the shapes. Arrange them in the order that makes sense to tell about the topic. Write your paragraph. On another sheet of paper, glue the shapes in a column to match the order in your writing.

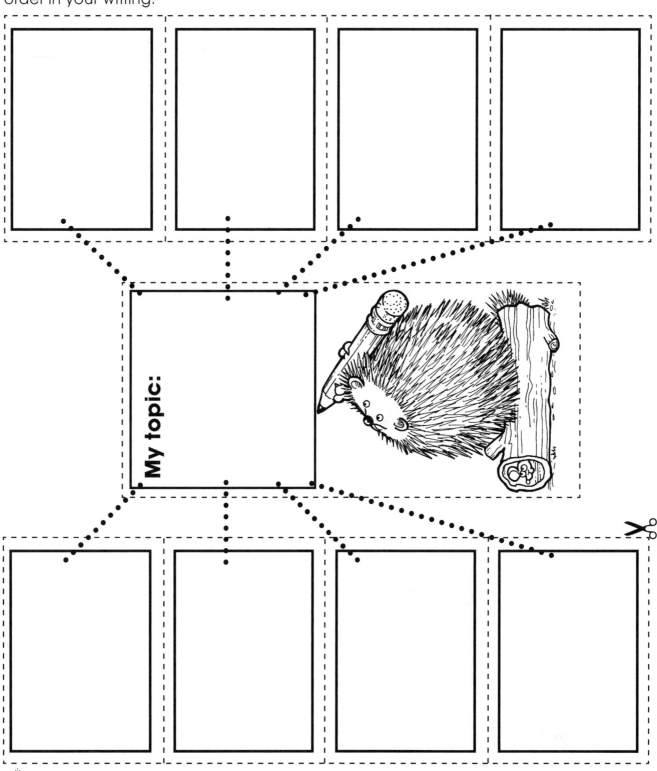

Name ——————————————

Use this tornado shape to help you find a good writing topic. Write a big topic in the space at the top. *Space*, *dogs*, and *friends* are big topics. Below it, write a topic that is smaller, like *Mars*, *poodles*, or *my friend Alex*. Do this step two more times to narrow the topic and fill in the bottom parts of the tornado.

Good writing topic!

Name _____

 Use this page to help you brainstorm. Write each event on a brick. Cut out the bricks. Put them in the order you want the events to happen in your writing. Glue the bricks onto a sheet of paper. When you write, follow the bricks to keep the events in the right order.

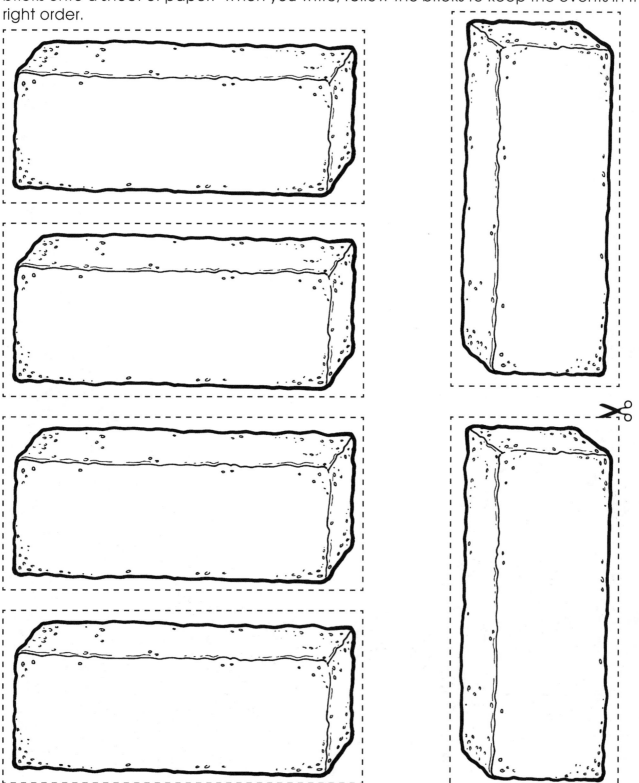

Stopping for Directions

Learning to write directions is a good lead-in for writing longer paragraphs and stories. It gives students practice with writing complete sentences and thinking about the order in which events occur. It is simple to fit writing directions into everyday class work because students have to follow so many different directions while at school.

Special Tips for Writing Directions

- Demonstrate different ways to format directions, such as using sequence words, ordinal words, numbering, and bullet points.

- Emphasize chronological order as you teach directions. Remind students that they need to record all of the steps in a process and arrange them in the correct order. To correct the order of directions, allow students to cut apart their papers and reorder directions by gluing the steps onto another sheet of paper. This will save time because students will not have to rewrite, and it also adds a kinesthetic element to the exercise.

Directions Reproducibles

- Revisit the **Brick Wall Organizer** (on previous page) and have students use it for writing directions. If you want to create a theme assignment, let students build something and write their building directions on the bricks.

- Have students complete the **Looking for Clues That Show Order** reproducibles (pages 70–72) to help them recognize certain words that can be used to put events in order. Before distributing the activity pages, let students review these vocabulary words on the board. Talk about how they can use some of these words instead of *and then* when telling their stories.

- Students must think logically to number the steps correctly on the **Directions in Order** reproducibles (pages 73 and 74).

- Use the **Recipe Card** reproducible (page 75) to have students record their favorite, simple recipes from home. Choose a few yummy, nonbake recipes to test in class and share.

- Have students follow the path in the **Getting Around at School** reproducible (page 76). After they have completed the maze, let them write directions for Reid to walk from the classroom to the playground. If students enjoy the assignment, make additional blank copies of the maze and have them write directions for walking from the playground, to the water fountain and so on.

- The **I Am an Expert!** reproducible (page 77) is a natural follow-up to the "expert sticks" activity (page 60) from the chapter Prewriting with a Purpose. Have students take home copies of this reproducible and discuss what they are very good at with their families. Examples might be putting hair in ponytails, making chocolate milk, or brushing their teeth. (They can also use ideas from their bundles of craft sticks from the expert sticks activity.) Once a student chooses a topic, have her write directions for it on the reproducible and draw a picture of herself performing her expert task. These are great reproducibles to publish in the classroom for a parent night, especially if you set up stations for student demonstrations.

- Make copies of the **Science Steps** reproducible (page 78) and have students work with partners planning and recording the steps of an experiment as they complete it. This is a good exercise to use when students are performing inquiry experiments.

Directions Activities

- The arrival of new students and staff members offers great opportunities for students to write directions. If a new student or staff member is coming to your classroom, pair students and have them write directions for walking from the classroom to specific places around the school or instructions for conducting certain classroom routines, such as morning meeting, roll call, going to the playground, or collecting lunch money. If you do not have a new person coming to school, let students write directions for getting around the school and following class routine. Then, keep these in a folder for substitute teachers.

- Writing directions to a fantastic place, either real or imaginary, can be a lot of fun. Students can generate directions for traveling to Jupiter, a secret cave, a princess castle, or anywhere else they can think of.

- Have students write directions for a simple task, such as making a snack, brushing teeth, using the telephone, or checking out a book at the school library. Each day, choose a different student's directions and follow them while the class looks on. Make notes on the student's paper of any roadblocks you hit while following the directions and then return the paper to the student so that he can make corrections.

Cross-Curricular Directions Assignments

- **Language Arts:** Different students have different ways of studying for spelling tests. Some write the words, some spell in the air, and some ask their parents to call out the words. Let students create sets of directions that tell how they study for spelling tests at home.

- **Math:** Writing directions for completing a math problem is a great exercise for students. It clarifies steps for them and also shows you where they need extra help. Assign some problems that represent math skills you are currently teaching; then, have students write or dictate the steps they took to solve the problems. Check that these and the answers are correct.

- **Social Studies:** Have students write complete directions for walking from their classroom to somewhere in the school, such as the cafeteria or the office. Let pairs of students follow a classmate's directions to see if they can reach the desired location. Some students, particularly those with special needs, may have great

difficulty with this exercise. Let those students say the directions while the class walks to that destination. Tape-record the directions; then, help the student write them later.

- **Science:** This is perhaps the most obvious subject area in which to teach directions. If you are able to seize on teachable moments to conduct science experiments, have students help create those experiments and write the steps they follow to test their hypotheses. You can also have students write directions for fun scientific activities, such as mixing cornstarch and water, dropping Mentos® candy into a soda bottle, mixing baking soda and vinegar, and other old favorites.

- **Science:** Copy some experiments from a student science book onto various colors of card stock. Cut apart the directions and discard the numbers for the steps. To make an answer key, glue a second copy of each selected experiment onto the inside panel of a color-coordinated file folder. Store the paper strips for each experiment separately in a zippered plastic bag. Place the bags in the reading area. When students have time between assignments, let them choose a bag and attempt to arrange the experiment steps in order by working independently or with a partner.

- **Physical Education:** Teach students a new playground game or let them play an old favorite.

When you come inside, as a class, write the directions for playing the game.

- **Physical Education:** When it is too cold or wet to go outside, start a calisthenics routine in your classroom. Teach students to do jumping jacks, sit-ups, stretches, lunges, and other age-appropriate activities. Do them in a certain order each day. Let students copy down the order and directions for the exercises onto file cards. Give each student a chance to lead the rest of the class through the designated exercises. Tell students they may follow their written directions to help them remember what comes next and how to do the exercises.

Evaluation Ideas

If you have students generate directions to follow in class, first test whether the directions actually work. If you do not have time to do this, enlist parent volunteers to help you test the directions. Whoever tests students' directions can easily give feedback about where the errors occur. Also, inform students that complete, correct sentences are important when creating directions because their writing needs to be very clear.

Name
</>

Name

Looking for Clues That Show Order **A**

Directions and stories happen in order. Some words help tell what that order is. Look at the clue words in the box. Dates and times are also good clues. You can use any of these words in your writing.

Examples of Clue Words

first	after	next
second	before	now
third	earlier	soon
fourth	end	then
fifth	finally	tomorrow
sixth	last	when
seventh	later	while

Read the paragraph. Circle **eight** words that tell you in what order things happened.

I went to my friend Casey's birthday party on Sunday. We ran an obstacle course at the end of the party. It was hard! We jumped over some benches. Then, we had to climb a rock wall. The  third thing we did was run around a tree two times. After that, we had to crawl though a tunnel. The last part was running through some tires. When we finished the tires, we got to ring a bell. I finished in fourth place. It was a great race!

70 KE-804078 © Key Education • *Make Writing Exciting!*
</>

Looking for Clues That Show Order B

Directions and stories happen in order. Some words help tell what that order is. Look at the clue words in the box. Dates and times are also good clues. You can use any of these words in your writing.

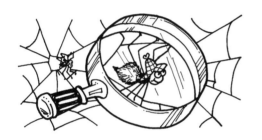

Examples of Clue Words

first	after	next
second	before	now
third	earlier	soon
fourth	end	then
fifth	finally	tomorrow
sixth	last	when
seventh	later	while

Read the paragraph. Circle **seven** words that tell you in what order things happened.

I got to stay after school to do an art project. First, I drew a picture of myself. I used crayons. Second, I colored the picture again to make the crayon very thick. Third, I covered the picture with black paint.

I had to wait for the paint to dry. Later, I scratched the paint off of the picture with a nail. This made the crayon colors show through the picture. Last, I put a paper frame around the picture. Next week, my parents will get to see my art at the class art show.

Name

Looking for Clues That Show Order C

Directions and stories happen in order. Some words tell what that order is. Look at the clue words in the box. Dates and times are also good clues.

Examples of Clue Words

first	after	next
second	before	now
third	earlier	soon
fourth	end	then
fifth	finally	tomorrow
sixth	last	when
seventh	later	while

Read the paragraph. Circle **nine** words that tell you in what order things happened.

My teacher brought caterpillars in a glass box to class. They changed a lot while we watched! First, they ate the plants in the box. They left big holes in the leaves. They soon started getting fatter. Then, they each made a hard case called a *chrysalis*. We watched the hard cases for ten days. Finally, the caterpillars came out of the cases. Now, they are butterflies! Tomorrow, we will let them go outside.

Directions in Order

 A

 Read the sentences. Number them in order. The first one is done for you.

1   This is how I make a banana split.

☐   Mom helps me scoop ice cream on top of the banana.

☐   I ask my mom to cut the banana in half.

☐   Next, I get out some ice cream, whipped cream, and a banana.

☐   I put the banana halves into the dish.

☐   First, I get a dish out of the cabinet.

☐   Then, I squirt whipped cream on top of the ice cream. Yum!

Name

Directions in Order

✏️ Read the sentences. Number them in order. The first one is done for you.

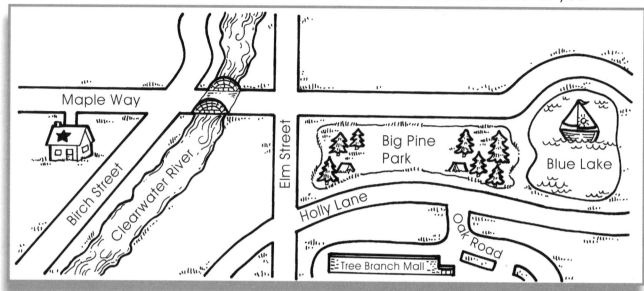

| **1** | This is how to get to the mall from my house. |

| ☐ | Turn right onto Oak Road. |

| ☐ | Ride east on Maple Way and turn south onto Elm Street. |

| ☐ | Turn right out of the driveway of my house onto Maple Way. |

| ☐ | Take the first exit from Oak Road into the Tree Branch Mall parking lot. |

| ☐ | Take Holly Lane until you reach Oak Road. |

| ☐ | From Elm Street, turn east onto Holly Lane. |

Name _____

Recipe Card Template

✎ Write a recipe for preparing a food you like. Write its name at the top of the card.
List the ingredients. Number and write the steps to make the food.

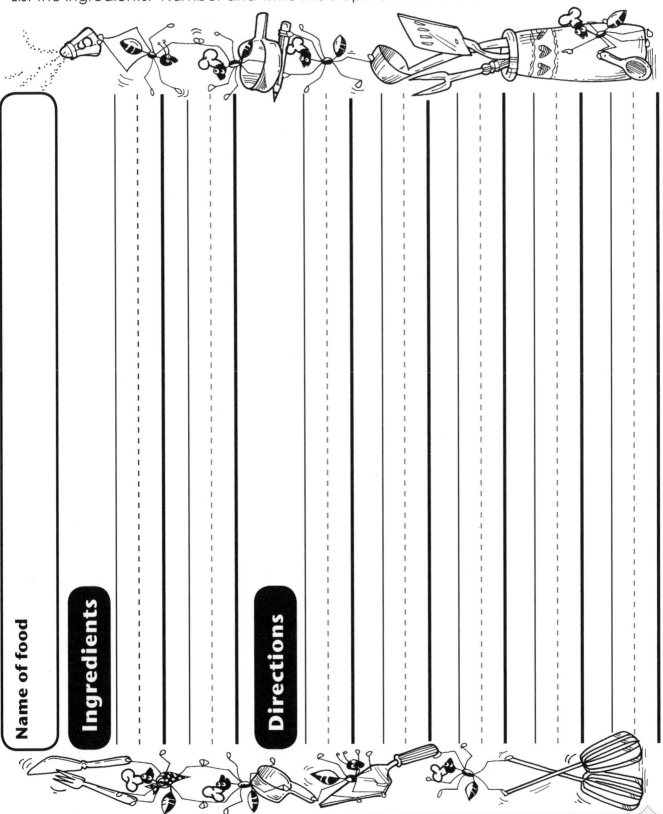

Name of food

Ingredients

Directions

Getting Around at School

Help Reid find his way from his classroom to the playground. Follow the path. Write directions for Reid to use next time.

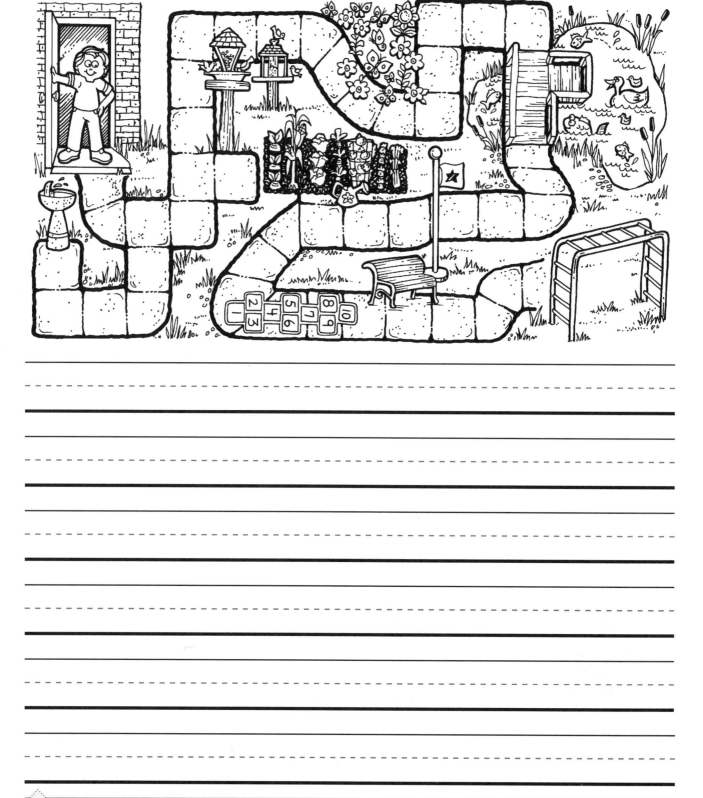

_____

_____

_____

_____

_____

_____

_____

_____

_____

_____

_____

Name

I Am an Expert!

✏️ Can you braid your own hair? Does your dentist say you do a good job when you brush your teeth? Can you ride a scooter? Think of something you do very well. Write directions for how to do it. Draw a picture of yourself in the frame doing your expert task.

Science Steps

Think of a new science experiment. Write a list of things you will need to do it. Plan the steps. Write them in the correct order so that you can try the experiment again. After you work the experiment, write about what happened.

Title

What You Need

What to Do

Number your steps!

What Happened?

Paragraph Power

Hopefully, after writing lists, sentences, and directions, students are getting comfortable with several different types of writing and can apply what they have learned to writing paragraphs. A paragraph can be fiction or nonfiction, and many students will write stories at this point. This chapter focuses more on nonfiction. Look for tips that are specifically for stories in the next chapter, Strong Stories.

Special Tips for Paragraph

- You may be seeing a big gap between the skill levels of different students in your classroom, especially if you have students with special needs. Some students may be ready to move to writing longer texts while others are still struggling to write sentences. Offer struggling students more practice with previously taught skills, but let them try their hand at writing longer pieces, too. Some students will "unblock" when they are allowed to write without having to master every skill leading up to paragraphs. Trial and error will help you learn how to meet the needs of each student.

- The writing period may need to be longer so that students have time to complete paragraph-length assignments. Students with special needs may require more flexibility with writing time limits.

- Now is a good time to use dictating. Students who are physically or otherwise limited from writing with ease still have plenty of important things to say. If students have trouble completing longer writing, recruit parent volunteers to act as scribes while students dictate their stories and paragraphs. It will take less time for a scribe to take dictation if the scribe is allowed to type on the computer.

- Before students do any paragraph activities, teach them to indent paragraphs by placing two fingers at the beginning of the first lines on their papers, starting the beginning sentences at that point. Explain that each new paragraph needs to be indented.

- Students will need to get used to working on sentences within their paragraphs. Revisit activities in the Chapter 2: Superb Sentences (page 28) to help them address issues on the sentence level in their writing.

Paragraph Reproducibles

- Use the **Underlining Paragraph Parts** reproducibles (page 83–85) to teach students that paragraphs need to have a beginning (introduction or topic sentence), a middle (body), and an end (conclusion). Distribute green, blue, and red pencils. Read the paragraph on page 83 aloud as a class. Let volunteers identify each part of the paragraph. Have students underline the topic sentence in green, the body in blue, and the concluding sentence in red. Then, pair students and have them complete the activity on page 84. Finally, encourage each student to work independently on page 85.

- The **Topic Sentence Match** reproducibles (pages 86 and 87) let students match topics sentences to their paragraphs. Again, students can do this as a class, in a small group, or individually.

- Before starting the **Body Sentence Sort** reproducibles (pages 88 and 89), teach the words *archerfish* and *telescope*. Give each student a copy of each page. Each student should cut out the detail sentences and then glue each one in the correct box near the matching topic sentence. Praise students if they arrange the sentences in an order that makes sense. To make this a class exercise, assign students to small groups and have them work together to arrange the sentences in order.

- One of these sentences is not like the others. Help students find out which one in the **Misfit Sentences** reproducibles (pages 90 and 91). Let students read the paragraphs and cross out the sentences that do not belong.

- In the **Write the Body** reproducibles (pages 92 and 93), students can practice writing the middle part of a paragraph between the topic sentence and the conclusion, which are both provided.

- Use the reproducibles **Choose the Best Ending** (page 94) and **Write the Ending** (page 95) to help students find effective endings to paragraphs. Remind students that concluding sentences are used to summarize the details written about topic sentences. The first two exercises let students choose from prewritten concluding sentences. The last two exercises let students write their own conclusions.

- Display one of the paragraphs from the **Paragraph in Training** reproducibles (pages 96–98) on the overhead or make a copy for each student. Let students brainstorm ideas for improving the paragraphs. Hopefully, you will get responses that you taught students in previous chapters, like adding details and combining and varying sentences, narrowing topics, and writing a better ending. Let each student choose one or two strategies and apply them as she rewrites the paragraph. Collect the paragraphs. Choose a few good examples to read aloud.

- Let students cut apart the sentence strips on the **Mixed-Up Message** reproducibles (pages 99–101). On sheets of paper, have them glue the sentences in order so that the paragraphs make sense. If you think students will need extra help with the project, make an enlarged copy of the activity page and then have the class arrange the sentence strips for the story. Otherwise, students may work in pairs.

Paragraph Activities

- Start out slowly with paragraph activities. Let each student try writing a paragraph about a recent activity. For example, have students describe getting ready for school in the morning or what they did after school the previous day. Remind students that they need to indent their paragraphs. Collect the paragraphs and respond to them. Give each student one suggestion for improvement and at least one compliment on her writing.

- Write the following sentences in a column on the board: *My pet could win a Best Pet contest. I went on a great vacation last summer. I have a few chores to do around the house. I love celebrating my favorite holiday. My best friend can always make me laugh. I remember three things that happened on the first day of school.* Tell each student to pick one of the given sentences and write a paragraph using it as the topic sentence. Allow students a few minutes to do some brainstorming and planning. Then, have them write at least three sentences that tell about the topic sentence and remind them to write the closing sentence.

- Do the same exercise as above but with concluding sentences provided. Write the following sentences in a column on the board: *It was the best day I have ever had! I hope we will always be friends. I knew I had found the perfect pet. It's what makes this holiday special to me. That is how I help around the house. I can't wait to go back!* Again, let students have a few minutes to brainstorm and plan; then, ask them to write topic sentences and three body sentences for the conclusions they chose.

- For additional reinforcement, let students identify the topic sentence, body, and conclusion in a preselected paragraph from a textbook or chapter book. Copy the paragraph for students and have them use colored pencils to identify the three different parts.

- Color is a great way to add description and detail to paragraphs. Give small groups of students a box of 64 crayons. Let students choose five crayons and write paragraphs using the names of the colors they chose as descriptive words. For an extra challenge, remove the basic colors: red, green, blue, white, black, etc.

- Play "Insert a Word." Have students complete a paragraph writing exercise in class. Ask them to skip every other line on their papers as they write. Next, tell them to insert a new word into every sentence they wrote. Teach them how to make the insert text mark (^). Tell them to write the mark under the place where they want to insert a word and then write the new word above the line. Point out that they can write any kind of word they want, as long as the sentence still makes sense. Help students compare their original paragraphs with their revised ones and to compliment them on their new word choices.

- Address how students can come up with good titles for their paragraphs. Look at a few works with titles, such as children's books and textbook chapters. Explain that sometimes, a title tells exactly what is in the book. Other times, the title is interesting but does not tell everything about the paragraph (or story) so that the reader is surprised. Ask students to take out a piece of previous writing and make up three possible titles for it. Over the next few days, let students take turns sharing their papers with partners and brainstorm possible titles. Offer feedback to students about which titles work for their paragraphs but emphasize that it is up to them to select what they think works the best. Repeat this activity when students learn about story elements.

Cross-Curricular Paragraph Assignments

- **Language Arts:** Provide art supplies. Select a paragraph from a picture book that describes a scene or a character's appearance. Do not show the picture that accompanies the passage. As you read aloud, let students draw what you are describing. Afterwards, reveal the picture and let students write a short list of how their drawings are like the illustration in the book and how they are different. Good books to read for descriptive passages include *In the Tall, Tall Grass* by Denise Fleming (Henry Holt and Company, 1991), *The Polar Express* by Chris Van Allsburg (Houghton Mifflin, 2004), *Owl Moon* by Jane Yolen (Philomel, 1987) and *Mr. Pine's Purple House* by Leonard Kessler (Purple House Press, 2005). Try to select books students have not read since they will remember the illustrations from old favorites.

- **Math:** After introducing and practicing a new math concept, have students write a brief explanatory paragraph describing how to do the math problem. Encourage students to pretend they are writing the paragraphs to help other students who do not understand the concept.

- **Math:** If a student is having trouble with a new math concept, have him write a short paragraph explaining why he thinks he is having trouble. Ask him to describe the places where he gets confused when working problems. This exercise will help both of you pinpoint exactly what he needs to do in order to understand the concept.

- **Social Studies and Science:** Work on topic and concluding sentences. Choose an expository paragraph from a textbook. Cover either the first or last sentence in the paragraph and let students read the remaining text and supply their own versions of the missing sentence.

- **Health:** As academic standards become more and more demanding, often less time is spent in active play. Ask students how they feel about the amount of time they spend running and playing outside. Let each student write a paragraph about ideas she has for incorporating more physical activity into the school day. Try to implement some of the new ideas.

Evaluation Ideas

If you have not already done so, develop the writing rubric by which you will evaluate and grade student writing. Use the reproducibles from Chapter 10: Revising with Relish and the Editing Checklist from Chapter 11: Convening with Conventions to help you decide what skills to evaluate. Remember to evaluate only what students have been taught and modify the rubric as students acquire more skills. Each time the rubric changes, make students aware of the changes in your expectations.

Underlining Paragraph Parts A

✏️➡ Read the paragraph.
- Draw a green line under the topic sentence.
- Draw a blue line under the body.
- Draw a red line under the conclusion.
- Write a title for the story.

Title

I love to ride in airplanes. The best part is the takeoff. The plane goes faster and faster down the long runway. Then, it lifts into the sky. The ride is smooth. I like watching the cars and buildings on the ground get smaller and smaller. Flying through the clouds is fun. Sometimes, it gets a little bumpy and we have to stay in our seats. Mom always lets me get a soda on the plane. That is a treat! On top of the clouds, the sun shines so brightly. It seems so close. The sky is very blue. When we get ready to land, I feel the plane start to slow down. The cars and buildings get bigger again. It is fun to touch down on the runway with a little bump. When we are on the ground, the cars are back to their normal size. The sun seems far away again. As soon as we get off the plane, I ask my mom, "When are we flying again?" I hope I get to fly again soon.

Underlining Paragraph Parts

B

✏️ Read the paragraph.
- Draw a green line under the topic sentence.
- Draw a blue line under the body.
- Draw a red line under the conclusion.
- Write a title for the story.

Title

My town is having a drought. It has not rained much for a long time. Farmers near my house have to water their crops a lot. Sometimes, there is not enough water. Some of their crops have died. People are not supposed to water their lawns. Our lawn is yellow and crunchy. We cannot wash our cars, either. My family's car is very dirty. There is a pond in our yard. The water in the pond is low. I can almost see the bottom. My family watches the news at night to find out if it is going to rain. For many days there has been no rain. Today, the newscaster said we would get some storms tonight. I am going to leave my window open. I want to hear the rain. If it rains, many things will be better in my town.

Underlining Paragraph Parts C

✏️ Read the paragraph.
- Draw a green line under the topic sentence.
- Draw a blue line under the body.
- Draw a red line under the conclusion.
- Write a title for the story.

Title

Last night, I got to watch my grandpa sing opera. My dad would not let me go until I turned six. He said operas are very long. He did not think I could sit still and be quiet. The opera last night was funny and silly. It was about a band of pirates. Grandpa was one of the pirates. At the end of the opera, the pirates decide that they do not want to be pirates anymore. They want to be nice. They were all happy at the end. I was happy, too. I cannot wait to watch my next opera. I hope I get to see my grandpa and hear him sing.

Topic Sentence Match

 Read each paragraph. Draw a line under the best topic sentence.

Story A   Last week I lifted a rock and found some funny gray bugs. They tried to run away. I touched one. It curled up in a little ball! Yesterday, I lifted a larger rock. I saw a salamander! It was black with yellow spots. The salamander ran away before I could touch it. There is a large, flat rock that leans against a tree in my backyard. I moved it today. Big, black ants came pouring out of the tree. I can't wait to find another rock to move!

1. Salamanders move very fast.
2. You never know what you will find under a rock.
3. Ants can make their homes in trees.

Story B

First, find a flat, smooth floor. Set the dominoes next to each other. Put the short end of each domino on the floor. The dominoes should stand up tall. Make sure they are close together. When one falls, it should hit the next one. Be careful not to bump them or you will have to start over. When you have set up all of the dominoes in a line, tap the first one gently. I like to watch them fall!

1. This is a fun way to play with dominoes.
2. I love to watch things fall over.
3. Dominoes and marbles are both easy to play.

Topic Sentence Match

Read each paragraph. Draw a line under the best topic sentence.

Story A
We walk along one of the big tanks and look through its glass walls. There are so many fish to watch at the zoo! It's fun to see their pretty colors. A school of butterflyfish swims by me. They are yellow and black. Their narrow snouts help them peck at food in small places. I see a bright yellow trumpetfish. It is a long, thin fish that does not look like a trumpet! Swimming above my head in another tank is a whale shark! It's the largest kind of fish in the sea. Many kinds of colorful fish swim in the tanks. I want to learn all of their names!

1. A large orange fish with blue dots also swims by.
2. There are many different fish to see at the zoo.
3. I hope to see a great white shark.

Story B
Most frogs live near ponds. The water-holding frog lives in the hot desert in Australia. Very little rain falls there. It's very dry. Most frogs need plenty of water to live. The water-holding frog needs very little water. This frog eats when it rains. It also drinks water. Soon, the water starts to dry up. The frog digs a deep tunnel with its back legs. It sheds its skin. It sleeps in the skin like a cocoon. The skin helps keep the water in the frog. The frog stays in the ground until it rains again. Then, the frog comes out of its hole. It will eat and drink until the water dries up. It will dig a new tunnel. The frog will wait until the next rain to come out again. Other frogs could never live there. The dry, hot desert is perfect for this strange frog.

1. Frogs like water.
2. It is hot in the desert in Australia.
3. The water-holding frog is a very unusual frog.

Name

Body Sentence Sort

Cut out the sentences on page 89. Glue them in the correct boxes.

Topic A

Look out for fish that spit!

Topic B

It can be hard to find a good place to look at the night sky with a telescope.

Name

Body Sentences for Sorting

Cut out the sentences below. Read the topic sentences on page 88. Sort the sentence strips. Can you arrange the sentences in an order that makes sense? Glue them in the correct boxes.

Finding a perfect spot for your telescope will be worth it.

The fish aims its tongue at the insect.

Find a place where trees will not block the sky.

When they find food, they swim under it.

Do not stand under a streetlight.

When the water hits the insect, it falls in.

Archerfish like to eat insects.

Try to stand on a deck or climb a hill.

They stick their mouths out of the water.

When you find a good spot on a clear night, you will be able to see the moon, many stars, and some planets.

Then, it spits water into the air.

It also helps to find a dark place.

They look for food on plants that are near the water.

Do not stand near a street or where you can fall.

The fish eats it.

Since it will be dark, stand in a safe place.

Misfit Sentences

Read each paragraph. Draw a red line through the sentence that does not belong.

Story A Polar bears live in the Arctic Circle where it is very cold. The bears have a thick layer of blubber. Blubber is another word for *fat*. The bears get the fat from eating seals. The fat keeps them warm. I like to wear a coat when it is cold. When it is very cold and windy, polar bears may dig holes in the snow. They hide in the holes until the storm is over. They cover their noses with their paws to keep warm. These bears are built for cold weather.

Story B

There are a few differences between hamsters and gerbils. Hamsters do not have tails. Rabbits have fluffy tails. Gerbils have long, soft tails. They look more like mice. Hamsters like to sleep all day. They wake up at night. Gerbils sleep at night. They play and eat during the day. Hamsters like to live alone. Gerbils like to be with other gerbils. Both gerbils and hamsters make good pets.

Misfit Sentences   **B**

Read each paragraph. Draw a red line through the sentence that does not belong.

Story A

Kangaroos can move not only by hopping but also by crawling. When looking for grass to eat, kangaroos stand on all four feet. Slowly, they crawl. They move their front legs together and then their hind legs. Sometimes, kangaroos need to move fast. Pushing off with their long hind legs, they bound across the land. As they jump, their short front legs are held close to their bodies. Their tails balance their weight. They live in groups called *mobs*. One kind of kangaroo can leap about 14 feet (4 m) in a single hop! It is fun to watch these animals move.

Story B

It is easy to tell when a storm is coming. Clouds gather in the sky. The sky starts to get darker and the clouds cover the sun. I like to be outside on a sunny day. The wind blows. It gets cool outside. Sometimes, it smells like rain. When thunder starts to rumble, it is time to go inside. The sound of thunder is quiet at first, and then it gets louder. Soon, you can see bright flashes of lightning before it thunders. Rain starts to fall, first slowly, then harder and harder. Sometimes, ice falls from the sky. The ice is called *hail*. Hail can be small like pennies or huge like baseballs. After the hail falls, the storm will usually start to move away. It stops raining. The thunder stops. The sun comes back. If you are lucky, you can see a big rainbow at the end of the storm.

Name _____

Write the Body

A

✏️ Read the topic sentence and the last sentence. Write sentences in between them to make a good paragraph.

This is what I do to get ready for school in the morning.

_____

- -

_____

- -

_____

- -

_____

- -

_____

- -

_____

- -

_____

After that, I am ready for school.

Write the Body

 Read and complete the topic sentence and the last sentence. Write sentences in between them to make a good paragraph.

_____ is my favorite activity. Here is how I do it.

And, that is how I _____.

Name

Choose the Best Ending

Read each paragraph. Draw a line under the sentence that makes the best ending.

Story A   My class is having an ice cream party. It is today after lunch. We invited our families. They will bring things to put on the ice cream. My dad is bringing sprinkles. My whole class cannot wait until the party.

1.   I like mint ice cream the best.

2.   We are excited to see our families and eat ice cream at school.

3.   We will eat pizza for lunch.

Story B   People all over the world do special things for their New Year. In Japan, people clean their houses. They put up bamboo and pine branches in front of their houses. In China, people pay back money that they owe. The adults give children red packets of money. Everyone enjoys the parades. People give gifts in France. In the United States, crowds count down to the New Year. Some people watch a glass ball drop as they count. In South Africa, there are fireworks and parties.

1.   The New Year is fun around the world.

2.   People in Brazil may wear white clothes. They eat lentils at a late dinner.

3.   Fireworks are fun to watch.

Write the Ending

Read each paragraph. Write a sentence that makes a good ending.

Story A

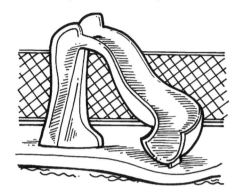

The best swimming pool in our town is Parkside Pool. It opens early in the morning. It has two water slides. One is very, very tall and one is small. I like the small slide better. It has a place where you can walk down into the water without having to use stairs. Lots of little kids play there. It has two big fountains. But, the best thing about the pool is the huge pirate ship. You can climb on it and walk the plank. Then, you jump into the water.

_____

- -

Story B

I had to go shopping with Grandma today. I do not like to shop. I said I did not want to go. She made me go anyway. First, we went to the mall. She bought a dress and a hat. Next, we went to the shoe store and she got two pairs of shoes. After that, we went to the market. She bought milk, bread, and soup. She let me pick out some candy to eat on the way home. That made me feel a lot better.

_____

- -

Paragraph in Training

A

✏️➤ Think of **two** ways to make the paragraph better. Write the new story below.

Guinea pigs make good pets. They are friendly and cute. They like to be held gently. They are small enough to sleep in a cage. They like to chew on things. They eat lots of vegetables and fruits. I like fruits, too. My guinea pig is named Harold.

KE-804078 © Key Education • *Make Writing Exciting!*

Paragraph in Training

Think of **two** ways to make the paragraph better. Write the new story below.

My dad runs a lot. He is going to be in a race. The race is on Saturday. The race is in a park. He has to run almost three miles. He thinks he will not win the race. He says he is not a fast runner. He says it does not matter if he loses the race. He says the important part is doing his best.

Paragraph in Training

 C

✏ Think of **three** ways to make the paragraph better. Write the new story below.

I wanted to paint my room a new color. I do not like the color it is now. I went to the store with my mom. We picked out new blue paint. We painted the walls.

Name

Mixed-Up Message

A

Cut out the sentences and the picture. Put the sentence strips in order so that the story makes sense. Glue everything on a sheet of paper.

Next, the music teacher took away one chair.

When the music stopped, we each tried to sit in a chair.

My friend Sam did not get a chair, so he was out.

The music teacher started the music.

We all walked around the chairs while the music was on.

I could not find a chair!

The teacher took away another chair.

I was out, too!

Since Sam was out, he got to start the music.

We walked around the chairs again.

Sam stopped the music.

First, we put all of our chairs in a circle.

Today in class, we played a game called Musical Chairs.

At least I get to start and stop the music next time.

Name _____

Mixed-Up Message

Cut out the sentences and the picture. Put the sentence strips in order so that the story makes sense. Glue everything on a sheet of paper.

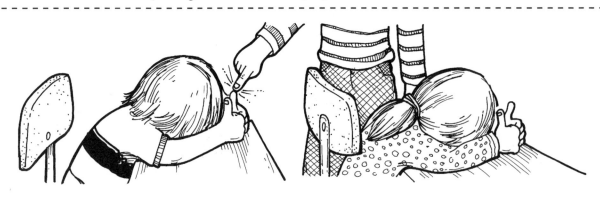

We put our heads down and hide our eyes.

We try to guess who tapped our thumbs.

If someone guesses right, she gets to trade places with the tapper.

Seven people stand in front of the class.

Each tapper walks around and taps one person on the thumb.

They are the tappers.

We play the game until the teacher says it is time to stop.

With our eyes shut, we stick out our thumbs.

When the tappers finish tapping, they go back to the front of the room.

If someone guesses wrong, the tapper stays up front.

My favorite game is Seven Up.

The rest of us sit at our desks.

Everyone whose thumb is tapped puts his thumb down.

KE-804078 © Key Education • _Make Writing Exciting!_

Name

Mixed-Up Message

Cut out the sentences and the picture. Put the sentence strips in order so that the story makes sense. Glue everything on a sheet of paper.

Then, the same person is "It" again.

If the Goose cannot catch "It," the Goose sits in the middle for the next game.

My sister Anna loves to play Duck, Duck, Goose.

Then, the Goose gets to be the new "It."

"It" walks around the circle.

When he says, "Goose," that person chases him around the circle and tries to tag him.

He says, "Duck," every time he taps someone.

One person gets to be "It."

You can see why this game is exciting!

"It" taps each player on the head.

If the Goose catches "It," "It" must sit in the middle of the circle for the next game.

She and her friends sit in a circle.

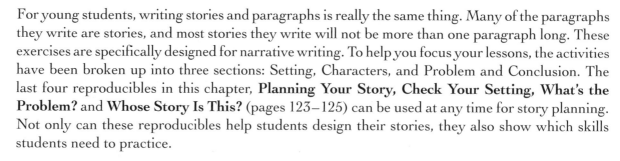

Strong Stories

For young students, writing stories and paragraphs is really the same thing. Many of the paragraphs they write are stories, and most stories they write will not be more than one paragraph long. These exercises are specifically designed for narrative writing. To help you focus your lessons, the activities have been broken up into three sections: Setting, Characters, and Problem and Conclusion. The last four reproducibles in this chapter, **Planning Your Story, Check Your Setting, What's the Problem?** and **Whose Story Is This?** (pages 123–125) can be used at any time for story planning. Not only can these reproducibles help students design their stories, they also show which skills students need to practice.

Setting

Setting Reproducibles

- Expand your setting discussions by having students complete the **Using Your Five Senses** reproducible (page 108). Take students to a variety of locations outside of the classroom, such as the playground, the cafeteria, or on a nature walk. Visit the location early in the morning and late in the afternoon. During each visit, let students fill out copies of the reproducible. Do at least one yourself and then copy your answers onto a piece of chart paper or the overhead. On the overhead, write a paragraph using the notes you made to demonstrate how to turn answers from the reproducible into a paragraph. Next, let each student choose one of the pages she has completed and use her notes to write a paragraph.

- Have students read the paragraphs on the **Seek Out the Senses** reproducibles (pages 109 and 110). Give each student a set of colored pencils or highlighters. Tell students to highlight places in the story with different colors where they see different senses being used: blue for seeing, green for hearing, yellow for feeling (touch), orange for smelling, and red for tasting. Consider enhancing the activity by serving chocolates and cinnamon rolls for snack while students do these writing assignments.

- Have students read the paragraphs on the **Where Am I?** reproducibles (pages 111 and 112). Students can answer the title question on the writing lines beneath each paragraph.

Setting Activities

- Explain that *setting* means where and when a story takes place. Share with students a few examples of locations where stories could take place, such as inside of a spaceship, under a rock, at the bottom of the ocean, or in the classroom. Then, discuss examples of when a story could take place, such as last week, 200 years from now, in April, at night, or at five o'clock in the afternoon. Let each student recall a favorite book and write a brief description of where and when the story took place. Conclude the activity

by having each student write details that show how he knows what the setting is.

- Set up "senses stations" to create a huge word bank. *Note: Be aware of any allergies your students may have.* For the **Touch Station**, find a fairly large box and cut a hole in the side of the box that is about 4 in. (10 cm) in diameter. Inside the box, place a few items that are interesting to feel, such as "gumballs" (seed pods from sweetgum or sycamore trees), feathers, and a small container of cornstarch and water. For the **Smell Station**, soak several cotton balls with different liquid scents, such as lavender soap, vinegar, mouthwash, and chocolate syrup. Push each cotton ball into the bottom of a small, plastic container and add a lid. Punch a few small holes in each lid. At the **See Station**, post items such as an inkblot, a famous artist's print, a piece of colorful fabric or wallpaper, and a microscope with a slide on it. If you can put the station near a window, provide binoculars. At the **Taste Station**, offer bite-sized pieces of foods with different tastes, such as a lemon, an apple, piece of chocolate, a pickle, a water chestnut, and a cracker. *(Note: Follow school guidelines for serving food.)* For the **Hear Station**, set up headphones, a player, and a recording of the following sounds: a bell, a whisper, some classical music, birds singing, and a machine operating. Near each station, supply a piece of chart paper and label it. As students move through each station, have them write three words that describe their experiences at the station. For example, a student might write *crunchy, sweet,* and *pucker* at the Taste Station. When students work on future writing assignments, display the chart papers around the room and encourage them to use words from the lists in their writing.

- Post a piece of butcher paper along with a piece of chart paper on a bulletin board. On the butcher paper, draw something that could be part of a setting, such as a tree. Then, write a sentence describing the tree on the chart paper, such as *A large, leafy tree grew in the middle of the meadow*. Ask a student to add one item to the picture (cow) and then dictate a sentence about her detail. *(Standing in the shade was a cow.)* Write her sentence on the chart paper. Let students continue to add details and dictate sentences. When several students have had a turn, ask a volunteer to read aloud the paragraph describing the scene.

- Help students learn how to set the scene using the works of some of their favorite writers. Provide art supplies for each student. Select a picture book or paragraph that includes a good description of a character or setting. Cover the book jacket and do not show the page illustrations to the children. On the first reading of the selected passage, have students listen. On the second reading, encourage them to draw pictures based on what they heard. As you read the passage aloud the third time, encourage students to think about how their illustrations compare to the pictures in the book. On the backs of their drawings, students can list three similarities and three differences. Finally, discuss how good descriptions helped them draw their pictures easily.

- When students are ready to write their own stories, hand out copies of the **Check Your Setting** reproducible (page 124). Have students answer the questions before paragraph writing as a brainstorming aid or afterward as a checklist. You may wish to group this reproducible with copies of **What's the Problem?** and **Whose Story Is This?** (See pages 124 and 125.)

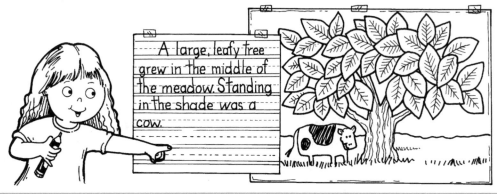

Characters

Character Reproducibles

- The **Character Hunt** reproducible (page 113) helps students identify characters in a story. Direct students to look for the names of the characters and fill in the blanks.

- Students can add their own characters to a story with the **Name the Characters** reproducibles (pages 114 and 115). Tell them to be careful when writing the names in the blanks. The blanks are numbered to help them. Invite a few students to read their stories aloud to see how they sound with different names.

- The **Character Planner** reproducible (page 116) helps students brainstorm details about their characters. Students will do more character work later on in this book, but this page introduces them to things they can think about in order to create a good character. Have each student finish the sentences and draw a picture of a character. For more focused practice, as a class, brainstorm a list of occupations, such as princess, dog trainer, clown, pilot, dancer, construction worker, race car driver, and deep-sea diver. Tell each student to choose one occupation and write it on the body shape. Then, let students complete the form and use the information to create characters for their own stories.

- Demonstrate the activity from the **Silly Faces** reproducible (page 117) on the overhead before giving students copies of the page. Ask a volunteer to draw a silly face on a piece of chart paper. Give the character a name. On the overhead, write a short story that tells about what emotions the character is feeling and why. Make the story elaborate so that students will follow your example and write more. For example, if a student draws a sad face, instead of writing *Bob is sad because his dog ran away*, write a full story about how Bob's dog ran away with the circus to become a performer but then invited Bob to come with him and be a circus performer, too.

This picture could show how Bob felt when his parents said, "No," but explain that later, they took him to the circus to visit his dog.

Finally, give each student a copy of the **Silly Faces** reproducible. Let each student choose a character from the reproducible and then write a short paragraph that includes the character's name and tells what the character is feeling and why. If interested, encourage students to complete the activity a second time by choosing a different silly face and writing a paragraph on another copy of the reproducible. After working with students on this activity, extend the lesson by challenging the class to draw and write paragraphs about other imaginary characters.

- The **Who Said What?** reproducible (page 118) will give students some practice with using quotation marks as they write dialogue. Younger children may not be ready for this skill, but older students should be able to understand how to set off what each character says. You may wish to pair students and have them take turns reading aloud the dialogue to reinforce what the characters are saying before adding the missing quotation marks. Alternatively, combine this reproducible with other activities that require students to write dialogue. *Special Tip: When you teach students about writing dialogue, explain that it should do two things. It should sound like real people talking and it should help move the story along.*

- When students are ready to write stories, let them fill out a **Whose Story Is This?** reproducible (page 125) as a brainstorming aid before writing their first drafts or as a checklist afterwards to see if more details are needed to describe their characters. It can be used in conjunction with the **Planning Your Story** reproducible (page 123) or **Check Your Setting** and **What's the Problem?** reproducibles (page 124) as a complete story planning activity.

Character Activities

- Do a classroom version of the **Silly Faces** reproducible. Photograph yourself and students making silly faces. Do not explain the purpose of the activity until you have photographed each student. Give each student a copy of a photo of himself or of another student. Let each student write a fictional story about why he is making a silly face. Write a story about your own photograph, as well. Encourage students to read aloud their stories and post them on a bulletin board.

- Students will often be characters in their own writing. Let them draw self-portraits. Then, have them write some things about themselves as characters in a potential story. Ask the following questions to get them started: *Describe what you look like. What's your favorite food? Name something you wish you never had to do again. What kind of person do you like to have for a friend? Describe something you are good at doing. List three things that have happened to you that would make a good story.* You may want to have students complete copies of the **Character Planner** reproducible about themselves before they write their stories.

- After students have written some stories, spend a little time reading each student's story with her. Ask her to tell you about the characters. Find out how old they are, what they look like, where they live, how they know each other, and other details about the characters, treating them as if they are real people. Alternatively, let students trade stories and encourage them to ask questions about each other's characters.

- Start teaching dialogue by using real dialogue. Pair students. Allow each pair to have a short conversation as you tape it. Try not to tell students what to talk about; just let the conversation happen naturally. If they seem to be having trouble, have them decide on a topic and then start recording the conversation again. Enlist some parent volunteers to transcribe the conversations. Give each student a copy of his transcription. Let each pair come to the front of the class and read the conversation aloud. This will give them practice seeing what dialogue looks like in print.

- It can be difficult to teach students to begin a new paragraph every time a different character speaks. When you start teaching dialogue, let students write stories in the **Who Said What?** reproducible style of writing, skipping a line between every sentence. Do not worry too much if students have trouble understanding how to format a conversation. At this stage it is much more important that students find good things for their characters to say, rather than formatting the dialogue correctly.

Problem and Conclusion

Problem and Conclusion Reproducibles

- Each student should look at the pictures on the **Picture Problems** reproducible (page 119) and write or dictate a problem that could be used in a story. Invite students to share their problems to see different ideas for the same picture.

- Use the **Solve the Problem** reproducibles (pages 120 and 121) to help students find and then solve problems in their writing. Direct students to highlight or underline the problem in each paragraph and then add a few concluding sentences for each. Students may also illustrate their solutions on the backs of their papers.

- The **Writing a Good Conclusion** reproducible (page 122) lets students find their own answers for a complicated problem. Have students write two possible conclusions.

- When students are ready to write stories, let them fill out copies of the **What's the Problem?** reproducible (page 124) as a brainstorming aid to help them plan their plots or as a checklist after writing their stories. Students may use the reproducible to determine if they explained their problems clearly and resolved them effectively.

Problem and Conclusion Activities

- Brainstorm a class list of problems and solutions. Go around the room and let one student name a problem. The next student should name a solution. List the problems and solutions on the overhead. When you are finished, compile the problems and solutions and make a copy for each student. Each student should then choose her favorite problem and solution and write a story around the selected prompt.

- Scan your local newspaper for possible problem-and-solution writing opportunities. If the articles are difficult for students to comprehend or too lengthy, have students base their work on headlines or photographs. The local news section often contains problems students will be able to understand. For example, you might find headlines such as: *Historic House Stands in the Way of Progress, Zoo in Need of New Alligator Habitat*, or *Budget Too Small to Build New Elementary School*. Cut out each article, headline, or picture. Glue it onto a larger piece of card stock and write a summary beside it. Have students state the problem and write/draw a solution. To extend the lesson, let students vote on their favorite solution and then send a class letter to the editor of the newspaper.

- After students have had some practice in writing stories with problems and solutions, let them trade papers and analyze other students' stories. On a separate sheet of paper, each student should write two sentences—one stating the problem in his classmate's paper and the other stating the solution. As the author, each student should read his classmate's analysis to see if the problem and solution sentences match what was actually written in the story.

Cross-Curricular Stories Assignments

- **Language Arts:** Use picture books to demonstrate good settings. Show a picture from the selected book that has a clear, detailed setting. Examples could be a scene from *The Mitten* by Jan Brett (Scholastic, 1990), the last scene from *Miss Bindergarten Gets Ready for Kindergarten* by Joseph Slate (Puffin, 2001), *Stranger in the Woods* by Carl R. Sams II and Jean Stoick (Carl R. Sams II Photography, 1999) or the last illustration in *The Napping House* by Audrey Wood (Harcourt Big Books, 1991). As you show the picture, let students call out words that describe the setting. Then, have them write paragraphs describing the setting using some of the brainstormed words.

- **Language Arts:** Read aloud a children's book about emotions, such as *How Are You Peeling?* by Saxton Freymann (Scholastic Paperback, 2004) or *Today I Feel Silly & Other Moods That Make My Day* by Jamie Lee Curtis (HarperCollins, 1998). Ask students to record some of the emotion words they hear in the story. Afterwards, ask students to choose one of the emotion words and draw a picture of someone who is feeling that emotion. Explain to students how their selected words inspired entire drawings. This is why authors should use good descriptive words to describe emotions.

- **Language Arts:** Picture books contain plenty of easy-to-find problems. Read aloud one or more of the following books and let students help find the problem. Then, have students predict the solution for the problem. When you finish reading a story, ask students these questions: "What was the solution for the problem?" "What happened to the character(s)?" "How did they feel about it?"

Examples include:

- ➤ *Don't Let the Pigeon Drive the Bus!* by Mo Willems (Hyperion, 2003). The pigeon wants to drive the bus, but the driver has said, "No."

- ➤ *Green Eggs and Ham* by Dr. Seuss (Random House, 1960). The nameless main character does not want to eat green eggs and ham, but his friend Sam really wants him to try it.

- ➤ *Kitten's First Full Moon* by Kevin Henkes (Greenwillow Books, 2004). Kitten thinks the moon is a bowl of milk that she just cannot reach.

- ➤ *Lilly's Purple Plastic Purse* by Kevin Henkes (Greenwillow Books, 1996). Lilly very much wants to play with her new purse, even though it disrupts the class and gets her into trouble.

- ➤ *Chrysanthemum* by Kevin Henkes (Mulberry Books, 1996) Chrysanthemum likes her long name until her classmates tease her.

- **Math:** To reinforce the idea of finding a math problem and a story in everything, share *Math Curse* by Jon Scieszka (Viking Juvenile, 1995). Have students practice identifying the problems and solutions in math story problems and restating them in their own words.

- **Physical Education:** Invite students to write stories that take place on the playground. Require them to include at least one piece of playground equipment in their settings. After the first drafts are completed, take the class outside and let each student walk through the action parts of her story. Give students time to implement the changes when they revise their papers.

Evaluation Ideas

As you read a student's story, consider whether it makes sense, whether it is well organized and told in a sequence that you can easily follow, and whether you want to know more about what the student is writing. All other issues can be easily fixed, but it is not so easy to make a dull story interesting or a confusing story clear. Focus on these issues above all else.

Name

Using Your Five Senses

✏️➔ Fill in the blanks. Describe where you are right now.

Place (where you are): ————————————————

Time of day (circle one):   morning   or   afternoon

What do you **see?**

What do you **hear?**

How does it **feel?**

How does it **smell?**

How does it **taste?**

Seek Out the Senses

✏️ Read the story. Write a title for it. Look for places where the people use their senses. Underline those words in the story:
- Draw a blue line for seeing.
- Draw a green line for hearing.
- Draw a yellow line for feeling.
- Draw an orange line for smelling.
- Draw a red line for tasting.

Title

My dad is from England. My brother Cole and I just flew over to visit my Gran for the first time. It is cloudy now that the plane is on the ground. The morning air is cool and damp. It smells like coal and cars. We get on the train to go to Gran's town. Gran drove to the train station to meet us. We hear her call out, "Hello, hello! I couldn't stand to wait for you at home!" She has chocolate in her pockets for us. It tastes very rich. She gives us big hugs. My face itches against her scratchy sweater. We put our luggage in her little car. Then, my dad says, "We can't all fit in the car. What should we do?" We try to fit into the car, but we are too big. Three people cannot fit. Dad does not want to make Gran walk. We can't walk by ourselves. Gran says, "Son, you drive home. The boys and I will walk!" Dad takes off in the rattling, noisy car. Gran says, "I walk this far every day. It is good for you." We have a good visit walking home with Gran.

Name

Seek Out the Senses

B

Read the story. Write a title for it. Look for places where the people use their senses. Underline those words in the story:
- Draw a blue line for seeing.
- Draw a green line for hearing.
- Draw a yellow line for feeling.
- Draw an orange line for smelling.
- Draw a red line for tasting.

Title

Ollie's Bakery is one of my favorite places. I love to go there early in the morning when it is still dark and cold. The lights were bright inside when I went today. I heard the bell ring as I opened the door. Miss Ollie usually comes to the counter to take my order. But today, she did not come to the door. Miss Ollie was not behind the counter. She was not in the back room with the big ovens. I was worried. I went outside and walked around the building. It was cold in the alley. Miss Ollie was sitting on a milk crate. She was feeding a bunch of cats. They sat around her and drank milk from little bowls. I could hear their tongues lapping the milk. Miss Ollie said she feeds the cats every morning. They were eating a lot today, so she was late for our visit. We went back inside together. Miss Ollie got my cinnamon roll. It smelled spicy. I sat down on a cold metal chair and picked up the roll. The roll was warm and soft. The icing was very sweet. When I finished, it was time for school. I walked to the door. I waved to Miss Ollie. She said she would let me help feed the cats tomorrow. I think Miss Ollie likes to feed anything that is hungry—like me!

 KE-804078 © Key Education • *Make Writing Exciting!*

Where Am I?

A

✏️➔ Read each story. Where do you think it takes place? Write your answer on the lines.

Story A

It was very quiet. I could not hear anything except for water. The water filled my ears. It was cool, but not cold. I waved to my mom. She waved back. She blew some bubbles. Her hair floated around her head. I saw some beautiful, yellow striped fish nearby. A ray swam under me. I hope our guide got some good pictures!

Where does the story take place? _____

How do you know? _____

_____

Story B

My feet crunched on the sticky floor. It was so dark. My bucket of popcorn was very hot. It smelled like butter. I felt the fuzzy backs of the seats as I walked. My friends followed me to the middle of a row. We sat down as loud music started playing. Lights came up in front of us. We were just in time!

Where does the story take place? _____

How do you know? _____

_____

Where Am I?

B

Read each story. Where do you think it takes place? Write your answer on the lines.

Story A

The black pavement under our feet is hot and soft. We walk as fast as we can, but our feet burn anyway. The car is very hot. Its seats burn us when we sit on them. I fold up my damp towel so that I can sit on it. My hair is still wet. My eyes are red. I am very tired and happy. I can still hear people splashing and sliding down the slide as we drive away.

Where does the story take place? _____

How do you know? _____

_____

Story B

The waiting room had a funny smell. I smelled it when I walked in. I heard buzzing and the sound of water. I saw the lady behind the window. My dad told her I was there. She said to wait a few minutes. I waited to hear them call my name. I read a magazine. When they called my name, I walked back to one of the little rooms. I climbed into the chair. I looked up into the bright lights and got ready to open my mouth.

Where does the story take place? _____

How do you know? _____

_____

Name _____

Characters in a story are just like actors in a movie. A story is about its characters. They can be people. They can also be animals. They can even be machines or cars or other things that act like people.

✏️ Read the story.

Umi-001

Mia and Matt jumped off the school bus and ran home. It was the last day of school. They were very excited. They could not wait to test their new robot! Mia and Matt had finished building it last night. It was waiting for them in Matt's room. All they needed was batteries for the remote control. They could not wait to have their own working robot. With any luck, it would clean their rooms for them.

"Matt, come on! We have to test Umi-001," said Mia. Matt ran after his big sister.

"Hi, Mom!" they called. Their mom turned around.

"I don't know what you kids did up there, but it's been very noisy today!" said their mom.

Matt and Mia looked at each other. What could have happened? They crept quietly to the door and opened it slowly.

"Hello!" said a strange voice. Matt jumped and Mia squealed. "I am sorry. I did not mean to alarm you." Umi-001 was rolling over to them with the remote in its hand. "Here, I fixed this for you. It does not need a battery now." Matt and Mia looked at each other. It was going to be an interesting summer!

✏️ Write the name of each character.

Character #1: _____   **Character #2:** _____

Character #3: _____   **Character #4:** _____

Name _____

Name the Characters

 Read the story.
- Use the key to fill in the blanks.
- Choose four names to use throughout the story. Write the names in the blanks.
- When you are finished, read the story out loud to a friend.

Character Key

1—boy's name
2—girl's name
3—family member's name
4—another boy's name

---

(1) _____ looked sadly out the window. Today was

the day someone new would move into his best friend's house across

the street. **(2)** _____ had moved out two weeks ago.

She did not want to move, but her **(3)** _____ had gotten a

new job in Denver. She promised to write to him.

"I will really miss you!" **(2)** _____ told him. "But, I will

send you postcards and letters."

"We can send you e-mails and pictures of where we live, too,"

said her **(3)** _____. "And, you can always come and visit.

It's only a couple of hours away." That had made **(1)** _____

feel a little better, but he still missed his friend.

Just then, the moving truck pulled up. A car was behind it. It was a

car just like his friend **(2)** _____'s! **(1)** _____ ran

Name the Characters (Cont.)

out of the house to see if his best friend had come back. But, the people who got out of the car were strangers. One of them was a boy about his age. The boy looked very sad. Then, he saw the boy watching him.

"Hello," said the new boy. "My name is **(4)** _____. We just moved here from Charlotte. It's a long way from here."

"I'm **(1)** _____. It's nice to meet you. My best friend used to live in that house."

"I guess you are not too happy that we moved in, then," said **(4)** _____. He looked worried.

"I miss her a lot," said **(1)** _____. "But, it's not your fault she left." The two boys stood there for a minute and did not say anything. Then, **(1)** _____ said, "Hey, do you want to play basketball when you are finished moving in? We have a hoop."

"That would be great!" said **(4)** _____. "I'll hurry and finish." **(1)** _____ thought maybe it wouldn't be so bad having a new neighbor, even if he still missed his best friend **(2)** _____.

Name _____

What does your character look like? Draw hair, a face, and clothing on your character. What do you know about your character? Finish the sentences as if your character is talking.

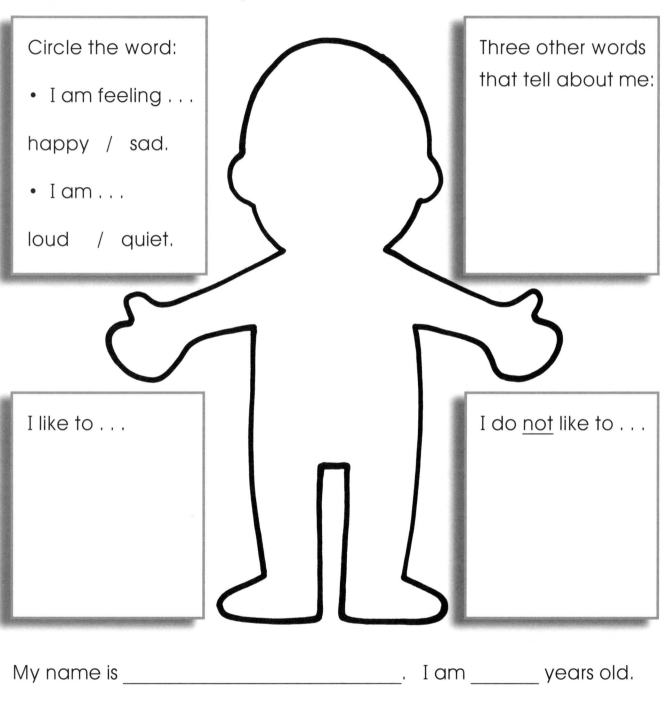

Circle the word:

• I am feeling . . .

happy / sad.

• I am . . .

loud / quiet.

Three other words that tell about me:

I like to . . .

I do not like to . . .

My name is _____ .   I am _____ years old.

I live on/in _____ .

In my family are _____ .

Silly Faces

Choose one of the silly faces below. Circle it. Write a story with this person as your main character. Choose a name for the person. Tell why this person is making a face.

Name

Who Said What?

Read the story. Look for places where Witt and Poppy are talking. Put quotation marks around the words they are saying.

Witt and Poppy wanted to play a game. I want to play checkers, said Witt.

We don't have a checkerboard, replied Poppy.

Can we play baseball? asked Witt hopefully.

I don't have a bat, said Poppy. Maybe we could jump rope.

Jumping rope is not very fun, sighed Witt.

Wait a minute! shouted Poppy. She ran into her bedroom. She came back with two rackets.

What are those for? asked Witt.

Let's go down to the park and play tennis! said Poppy excitedly.

Do you have tennis balls? asked Witt.

No, I guess not. Sorry. said Poppy sadly.

My brother has some, said Witt. Let me run to my house and get them!

I will meet you in my front yard, said Poppy.

Name

Picture Problems

✏️➤ Look at each picture. Make up a problem that could be happening in that picture. Write about the problem on the lines.

A

_____

- -

_____

_____

- -

_____

_____

- -

_____

_____

- -

_____

B

_____

- -

_____

_____

- -

_____

_____

- -

_____

_____

- -

_____

Name _____

Solve the Problem

A

Read the story. Find the problem. Draw a line under it. Add a few lines to the end of the story to solve the problem. Then, write an interesting title for the story.

Title

Kevin and his mom had a busy day at the mall. Kevin got to ride the carousel. His mom bought a new skirt. She got Kevin a shirt. He pushed the buttons on the elevator. They even had ice cream cones. They decided to walk to the car and drive to see a movie. Kevin's mom walked out the door and stopped. "What's the matter, Mom?" asked Kevin.

"I do not remember where I parked the car," said his mom. Kevin wondered how they would ever find the car.

_____

- -

_____

- -

_____

- -

_____

- -

_____

- -

_____

 KE-804078 © Key Education • *Make Writing Exciting!*

Solve the Problem

 B

✏️➤ Read the story. Find the problem. Draw a line under it. Add a few lines to the end
of the story to solve the problem. Then, write an interesting title for the story.

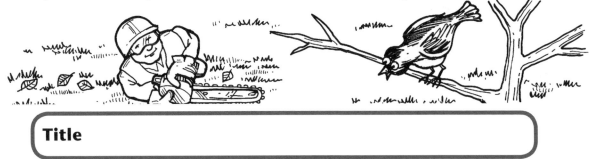

Title

   Ross, a busy robin, carried a few more pieces of straw to the new

nest. He and his wife were almost done building it. She was getting

ready to lay eggs. They wanted a safe place for their eggs to hatch.

They had put the nest in a tall tree. Ross saw a man walking over to

the tree. The man had a saw. Oh, no! The man was going to cut

down the tree! They had worked so hard on the nest. Ross did not

want the man to mess up their hard work. He came up with a plan.

Writing a Good Conclusion

✏️ Read the story. Find the problem. Write two endings that fix the problem. Circle the one you like the best. Rewrite the story on another sheet of paper. Draw a picture and give the story a title.

It was just two weeks to Abby's birthday. Her mom was going to let her have a birthday party at the mini-golf park. Abby loved to play golf!

Her mom told her, "The park can have parties for up to five people at a time. You can invite three friends." Abby counted.

"But Mom, that's just four people. I want to invite Jen, Anna, Kate, and Toni. We do everything together at school! Why can't I invite four friends?"

Her mom said, "Because your little brother will want to come. You can't leave him out." Abby did not know what to do. She did not want to leave out one friend, either. If she did not invite all four girls, one of them would be so sad. But, she had to invite her brother. If he could not come, he would be sadder than anyone!

Ending A _____

_____

_____

Ending B _____

_____

_____

Name

Planning Your Story

Use the 5 Ws *(Who, Where, When, What,* and *Why)* and the word *How* to plan your story. Answer the questions below. Then, write your story on another sheet of paper.

Who is in your story?

Where does it take place?

When does it take place?

What happens in your story? (Explain with a few words.)

Why does the main event in your story happen?

How is the problem fixed?

Check Your Setting

✏️ Think about the setting of your story. Answer the questions.

What time of day does your story take place? _____

What time of year is it? _____

Where does the story take place? _____

✏️ List one detail for each of the senses. Put these in your story, too.

Seeing: _____   Smelling: _____

Hearing: _____   Tasting: _____

Feeling: _____

- -

What's the Problem?

✏️ Think about the problem in your story. Answer the questions.

What is the problem in your story? _____

_____

Who will solve the problem? _____

How will it be fixed? _____

_____

Name

Whose Story Is This?

> Draw a picture of each character. Write the character's name. Then, write three words that describe the character.

Character 1

Name: _____

Description: _____

Character 2

Name: _____

Description: _____

Character 3

Name: _____

Description: _____

Character 4

Name: _____

Description: _____

Character 5

Name: _____

Description: _____

Passing Notes (and Letters and E-mail)

Nothing focuses writing like an audience, and nothing implies an audience like writing a letter or an e-mail. Many children who would never have seen their parents write anything 15 years ago now see them write daily e-mails, text messages, and blogs. Let students emulate their parents with some activities based on correspondence.

Special Tips for Notes, Letters, and E-mail

- If possible, provide computer access for students to practice writing letters and e-mails, even if they cannot send real e-mails from class. If they learn to associate being on the computer with writing instead of playing games, they may spend some time at home composing letters.

- Ask families to send in notepad remnants and leftover stationery and envelopes to inspire students to write notes and letters.

Provide colored pencils and gel pens to use with the paper.

- With young elementary students, you may not have to worry about text messaging abbreviations creeping into their writing, but if students have older siblings or parents who text a lot, they may want to use them. Decide ahead of time whether to allow abbreviations such as those used in text messaging.

Notes, Letters, and E-mail Reproducible

- Use the **Friendly Letter Template** reproducible (page 128) to help students learn letter formatting as they write letters to friends, family, and their teacher.

Notes, Letters, and E-mail Activities

- Here is the easiest writing assignment ever. Pass notes in class! Write each student's name on a slip of paper and then put the slips in a box. Let each student write a little note to the classmate whose name she draws. Do this often and encourage different topics: what students did over the weekend, their favorite subjects in class, how they are feeling that day, and so on. Let each student respond to the note he receives. To add fun to the activity, help students search out some creative ways to fold notes, like cootie catchers and paper airplanes.

- Let students decorate and personalize their own cards for birthdays and holidays. Give

each student a piece of construction paper folded in half (like a burger bun). Have each student draw art on the front of the card that corresponds to a current holiday. On the insides of the cards, students can write brief messages and sign their names. Then, deliver the cards to a younger class or a senior center.

- If students are still into pretending, provide a phone, notepad, and pencil; then, let students pretend to take messages for each other. You can prerecord some messages for students to listen to while they "talk" on the phone. This activity teaches students to paraphrase, summarize, and listen for details.

Have students "invite" each other to a birthday party where they are going to exchange "gifts." Provide blank invitations for students to fill out. Assign each student a classmate to invite to the party. After invitations are distributed, encourage each child to shop for a "gift." Provide toy catalogs. Have each student cut out a picture of the toy he would like to give as a gift, glue it on an index card, and then write a description of that toy. Randomly hand out the completed gift cards during class and let students write thank-you notes for their cool gifts using real thank-you cards and envelopes.

Periodically, provide students with opportunities to type letters on the computer instead of writing them. For a short assignment that is always relevant, direct students to write letters to their families describing what they did that day. Print out the letters on some special paper or have students decorate their letters by using stamps and ink pads. When each student sees her family and is asked the question, "How was school today?" she can hand over the letter as a response.

Let each student write a note to his parents, reminding them of an upcoming field trip or class event. Have parents sign the notes for students to return to you.

Cross-Curricular Notes, Letters, and E-mail Assignments

- **Language Arts:** Stop reading aloud a passage at a critical point in a book and have students write a letter to one of the characters, offering advice on what to do next.

- **Language Arts:** Have each student write a letter to a favorite author. Mail the letters if possible.

- **Math:** When students are working on story problems, have them write short explanations about how they solved them. Not only will students gain writing practice, but you will gain a better understanding of your students' mathematical reasoning skills. At times, supply students with more difficult problems to find out what strategies they would use.

- **Social Studies:** If your class is studying historical figures, have students write letters to them offering advice, asking questions, thanking them for certain inventions, and so on.

Evaluation Ideas

Although letters should usually be informal, the messages need to make sense. Have students adhere to the same conventions they have to follow for other assignments.

Name

✏️ Fill in this form to write a special letter to a family member or friend.

Expository Expo

A lot of student writing will be in the form of reports. In the primary grades, students should practice a more formal style of writing and also learn to put factual information in their own words.

Special Tips for Information and Reports

- Keep your expectations for students' reports realistic. Focus more on guiding them through the process of report writing than the excellence of the final product.

- It is crucial to teach the formatting you expect for each subject area. If you expect students to turn in specific parts of a book report, create a checklist so that students can fill in those parts. If you want students to write up a science experiment, note the sections you expect on a handout for students to follow later. Make your expectations entirely clear and easy to reference.

- Summarizing informational articles and explaining processes are common writing test prompts, so cover these in class. Although student writing tests may be a few years away, it is important for students to hear the terms and begin to use them in their speaking vocabularies.

Information and Reports Reproducible

- Use the **Book Review** reproducible (page 131) to simplify the book report process. With guidance, students can fill in the blanks to create book reports. Complete some summarizing activities (see below) with students so that they will know how to fill in the What happened in this book? section.

- Teach the art of summarizing. On the board, write the following summaries of fairy tales:

  ► Three pigs find out how to build a house that can even stand up to a wolf.

  ► Little Red Riding Hood learns that taking short cuts through the woods is not a great idea.

  ► Goldilocks surprises three bears who went out for a walk.

- You can also read summaries on children's book jackets, although they may be less complete than you like. After sharing several summaries, encourage each student to write a summary for a recently read book or article. Ask students to limit their writing to one or two sentences and to include only the main ideas.

- Do not limit children's experiences with writing summaries only to stories. Help students practice summarizing nonfiction articles and long textbook paragraphs. Read a passage aloud as students follow along. Ask a volunteer to name the main idea of the article and record it on chart paper as the topic sentence. Choose another volunteer to write the three most important details in the article on the chart. Ask a third volunteer for a conclusion, which is also recorded. Finally, compare the article and its summary. Ask students how they are alike and different.

Cross-Curricular Information and Reports Assignments

- **Language Arts:** Use the **Book Review** reproducible to create a yearlong writing project. As each student finishes reading a book from the classroom library or one brought in from home, have her fill in a copy of the reproducible. Store the completed forms in a folder in your reading area and let students read the book reviews when they are looking for new books to enjoy.

- **Social Studies:** Make a biography template by writing the following items on a sheet of paper: *Name* (of subject), *Birth date, Date of death, Birthplace, What this person is most famous for, Tell about the life of this person, How did this person change the world?* and *Draw a picture of this person.* Students can use the template to create fairly detailed biographies of historical figures.

- **Science:** Challenge students to create fact sheets about certain animals. These writings could be on animals that live in a certain biome (rain forest, desert, coral reef, or grassland) or belong to a specific animal group (mammals, fish, birds, reptiles, or amphibians). Design a template for students to complete or have them individually write a paragraph about a chosen animal. To build interest in the project, let students post drawings of the featured animals with their written work in a classroom display.

- **Science:** Create a science report template with headings like: *Experiment name, Materials, Results, Were the results what you expected? Why or why not?* and *Draw a picture of your experiment.* Use it with the **Science Steps** reproducible (page 78) from Chapter 5: Stopping for Directions.

Evaluation Ideas

If you expect students to know how to summarize, evaluate this skill. Check to see whether students have followed instructions for formatting and if the information they included is correct, relevant, and sufficient.

Name _____

Book Review Form

Fill in the blanks to tell about your chosen book. On another sheet of paper, draw a picture of your favorite scene in this book.

Title _____

Author _____

Characters _____

Setting _____

What happened in this book?

_____

_____

_____

_____

Did you like this book? Tell why or why not.

_____

_____

_____

Revising with Relish

Revising can be frustrating for students and teachers. When students write, they tend to see no need for revision, and it is difficult to explain the merits of rereading and changing text. Wording your comments carefully makes a big difference, so avoid questions with yes-or-no answers. For example, don't ask "Is this the best story you can write?" Without a clear plan for improvement, students are likely to say, "Yes." Note that the reproducibles **Make Your Paragraph Better** and **Make Your Story Better** are not open-ended, which makes each one more of a worksheet than a checklist, but these checklists also help students focus on how to improve their writing.

Special Tips for Revising

- Help students equate rewriting with revising but make it inviting for them. When they revise, give them colorful paper and pencils. Play music. Let them work in a different seating arrangement. Allow each child to choose a piece of candy from a basket or chew sugarless gum when she rewrites. If you make revision time a treat, students are more likely to approach it with enthusiasm.

- Note that all of the revision checklist reproducibles (pages 134–136) have bursts or stars for bullets rather than numbered lists. You can cover any item on the list before copying it for students. This allows you to address the problems your class needs the most assistance with first.

- Having to revise something on which they have already worked so hard can be frustrating for students with special needs and younger students with limited writing abilities. Ask parent volunteers to take dictation for some revision projects and allow more time for these students to complete their work.

Revising Reproducibles

- Use the **Make Your Paragraph Better** reproducible (page 134) to help students evaluate the major points in their nonfiction writing. Young students or students with special needs may need fewer criteria to stay focused and not become overwhelmed. To shorten the assignment, simply cover the listed items you do not want students to use before photocopying the page. Explain that sometimes writers will revise pieces that are not so good, but many times, writers choose to revise work that is already good because they enjoyed that piece and they want to make it even better. You may need

to offer guidance about which written work students should revise. Encourage students to choose pieces they still like to read or that were fun to write.

- The **Make Your Story Better** reproducible (page 135) is designed for stories. Use the same method as **Make Your Paragraph Better**.

- The **Help Your Friend Revise** reproducible (page 136) helps students learn how to critique each other's written work. The questions are meant to elicit positive comments and helpful suggestions.

Revising Activities

- Meet with students individually to talk about their written work. Before students revise, offer suggestions for which pieces of writing they should analyze. After students fill out checklists or otherwise think about how they would like to revise their written pieces, you can talk with them about their choices. Most students will welcome this special attention and use the discussion to form a plan of action. Plus, it will benefit students who are aural learners or who need the reinforcement gained from using more than one learning style.

- Emphasize the positive aspects of revision by making it a reward. Ask students to look back over their written work and choose three pieces they might like to revise. Read each student's choices. Choose one that you think would benefit from revision; then, put a big sticker on it along with a couple of positive comments. Return students' papers and encourage them to start revising.

- Have each student revise a written piece line by line. Each sentence will then have to stand on its own. Students can look for word choice, details, and flow within each sentence without being distracted by the flow of the paragraph as a whole.

- Explain that revising is different from proofreading. *Proofreading* means correcting grammar, spelling, and punctuation in their writing. *Revising* means making sure they said what they wanted to say in the way they wanted to say it. Comparing items on the **Make Your Paragraph Better** and **Make Your Story Better** to the **Editing Checklist** (page 139) will help them differentiate between the two things.

- Having students write for different audiences can help them see different ways to revise. To use an audience as the motivator for revision, get silly. Before students start revising, tell them to imagine that someone besides you is going to read the work. You can tailor the new readers to each individual student or offer some blanket choices. Ask how they would change their writing if their parents were going to read it? A policeman? The principal? A porcupine? A friend who is not in their class? Have students write the names of new audiences at the tops of their papers and then write three ways that the named audience would cause them to change their writing. Let them write their revisions to address their new audiences.

- Provide the same resources students used when they first wrote their papers. Let them revisit the word bank, look over research again, reread the picture book, etc. Looking at these resources when they already have their pieces of writing in hand can help them find mistakes.

Evaluation Ideas

- Review any checklists or notes students filled out before they wrote and see whether they incorporated the changes they planned. As students get more skilled at revision, you may also want to consider whether the piece was actually improved.

- Be careful when giving feedback for revisions. If a student was not very clear on reasons for the revision, any criticism may feel like he simply did a poor job of guessing what you wanted. Offer plenty of praise where students have succeeded with revision.

Name

Make Your Paragraph Better

✎⟶ Choose a piece of writing to revise. Read it out loud. Think about each question and then color its star. Your answers will help you decide how to make your writing better.

☆ What is the main idea of the paragraph? Is there a topic sentence?

☆ Are the sentences in an order that makes sense?

☆ Are there any sentences that do not belong?
(Cross them out if you have any.)

☆ What senses did you use? Check the boxes.

☐ seeing   ☐ feeling   ☐ smelling

☐ hearing   ☐ tasting

☆ Have you used four or five details to tell about your topic? Do you need to add more details? If so, where should you add them?

☆ Underline some interesting words that you used in your writing.
Are there any words that need to be changed?

☆ Does your paragraph have an ending sentence?
Can you make it more interesting?

☆ Does your title make people
want to read more?

Name

Make Your Story Better

Choose a story to revise. Read your story out loud. Think about the questions. Your answers will help you decide how to make your writing better.

 Why?　Why did you choose to revise this story?

 Topic　What is your story about? Is there a topic sentence?

 **Order**　Did you tell the story in an order that makes sense?

 **Characters**

- Did you tell enough about your characters?

- Do the characters talk to each other?

 **All belong?**　Are there any sentences that do not belong? (Cross them out if you have any.)

 **Interesting words**　Underline some interesting words that you used in your story. Circle any words that need to be changed.

 **Problem**

- What is the problem in your story?

- Was the problem solved?

 **Title**　Does your title make people want to read more?

Name

Help Your Friend Revise

✏️⟶ Read the story out loud. Answer the questions. Your answers will help your friend decide how to revise the writing.

☆ Title of the story: _____

☆ What do you think is the best thing about this writing?

_____

_____

_____

☆ What is the topic sentence?

_____

_____

☆ What is one thing that could be changed to make the writing better?

_____

_____

_____

☆ What did you learn from the writing?

_____

_____

_____

☆ What is your question for the writer?

_____

_____

Convening with Conventions

This is the phase of the writing process where students edit their papers for conventions—the standards for grammar, punctuation, spelling, and paragraph formatting that make writing readable. Proofreading for conventions is often the easiest job for teachers and sometimes for students, too, because it generates concrete changes that need to be made.

Special Tips for Editing and Proofreading

- Teach students that conventions are in place so that others can read their papers. Nonstandard spelling, missing punctuation, and confusing grammar make it hard for others to read their papers.

- It is important for this stage to come last. If students have many mistakes marked on their papers, it can discourage them from changing anything else.

- Limit proofreading to the things you have expressly taught students. Ask students to keep checklists of what skills they have learned. Only have them proofread for those things in their papers.

- Most writers swear by their editors and proofreaders. It is often very difficult to objectively correct something you have seen many times. Encourage students to ask family members and friends to read their papers and help point out errors. You may want to issue some guidelines to parents beforehand so that they offer the right amount of help. A list of questions for parents to ask their young writers will help make your expectations clear. Ask students to turn in all drafts so that you can see how much help they are getting.

- Let students with special needs, especially those who have dyslexia and dysgraphia, take advantage of typing on the computer and using spell-checker when possible. Also, allow students with special needs to read their papers aloud while editing or to look only for one type of mistake at a time. All of these tricks will help them stay focused and not feel overwhelmed.

- Especially toward the end of second grade, some students may wish to manipulate conventions for effect. For example, a student may start his paper with a list of descriptive words or include a fragment to emphasize a point. If you recognize a device like this in a paper, discuss it with the student to make sure it is intentional.

Editing and Proofreading Reproducibles

- Revisit earlier lessons in this book, such as the reproducibles from Chapter 2: Superb Sentences to refresh students' memories about those skills.

- Use the **Editing Checklist** (page 139) to help students focus on one type of mistake in their written work at a time. If needed, cover the items you have not yet taught with a piece of paper before copying the checklist and uncover them when necessary.

- The **Proofreaders' Marks** reproducible (page 140) shows the most common marks students in grades K–2 will use to correct their papers. If students seem ready, add to this list.

- Use the **Editing Treasure Hunt** (page 141) to make editing fun. To simplify the activity, cover the items on the lid that are not needed before copying the page. Reward students for how many mistakes they find. This exercise is effective with peer editing as well as self-editing.

Editing and Proofreading Activities

- Let students exchange papers frequently. Have them use copies of the **Editing Checklist** or the **Editing Treasure Hunt** while proofing their classmates' papers. After they have practiced with the editing tools several times, let them proof without using a reproducible to see if they have learned the rules.

- Write a paragraph that contains only the types of mistakes you have taught students to proof for. Distribute copies for students to correct. Display a copy on the overhead and identify the errors as a class. Use this assignment to introduce proofreaders' marks as you correct the paragraph.

- Use informal journal writing to create formal, published writing. Let each student choose a piece from her journal to take through the writing process. Toward the end of the process, focus on formatting and then editing.

- Show students how to check their corrections. As each student is rewriting his paper and making corrections, have him draw a line through each mistake with a highlighter or watercolor marker after changing it on the new copy. Once he is finished, he or another student can look back at each highlighted change to make sure the correction was made.

Evaluation Ideas

- In general, teach students to apply the appropriate formatting rules to the different subject areas. Review the formats with them each time students tackle a piece of writing.

- In order to keep proofing mistakes from taking over a student's final grade, predetermine how much weight editing has within the scoring of the paper. Unless you are grading only for editing, keep the total weight of this stage of the process to 15 percent or less. This will encourage students who are good at other things (such as generating ideas) but need more practice with editing to continue to work hard. It will also help keep students whose writing is correct, but otherwise lacking interesting sentences, from relying too much on having good grammar. As you near the end of the school year and student writing is improving overall, you can increase the weight of the editing portion of their grades. Make students aware of any changes in how you will grade their written work.

Editing Checklist

Read the list below. Draw a check mark in the box after you look for each item in your writing.

☐ My name and the date is on my paper.

☐ My writing has a title.

☐ The paragraphs are indented.

☐ Each sentence starts with a capital letter.

☐ Names of people and places start with capital letters.

☐ Every sentence has a **.** or **?** or **!** at the end.

☐ I have checked that my words are spelled correctly.

Name

Proofreaders' Marks

Mark	What It Means	Example
≡	Make this a capital letter.	j̲u̲l̲y is the best month.
/	Make this a small letter.	I like it when Ꞩummer comes.
———	Take out words or sentences.	Sometimes we ~~and~~ drive to the beach.
∧	Add words.	small, unbroken I look for ∧ shells.
⬭	Fix the spelling.	Playing in the (oshen) is exciting.
⊙	Add a period.	I want to learn how to surf⊙

 KE-804078 © Key Education • *Make Writing Exciting!*

Name

Editing Treasure Hunt

Ahoy, Matey! Let's search for mistaken treasure! On this treasure hunt, circle marks the spot! Read the piece of writing. Color a coin for each mistake that you find! Arg!

change to a capital letter.

Change to a Small letter.

Add ending punctuation⊙

Take out this of word.

Check your spieling.ˢᵖᵉˡˡⁱⁿᵍ

Proud to Be Published

Publishing is the culmination of brainstorming, writing, revising, and editing. When students have taken a piece of writing through all of the preparation it needs to be called "final," it is considered published. Published writing should not be writing that is being shared for the first time. Students should be used to having you and fellow students read drafts. But, it should be writing that, for whatever reason, students are proud enough of having written to take it to the publishing stage.

Special Tips for Publishing

- Published work should have a title. If students have not titled their work, they should do so before publishing. Encourage students to receive feedback from fellow students about the titles for their work.

- Every published piece of writing does not have to have a cover. Let students try several different publishing ideas.

- At least once, invite parents into your classroom to see student writing. Because the writing process has so many steps, students will naturally be proud of finished pieces and will want to show them off. Writing isn't as flashy as artwork on your walls, perhaps, but it can be one of the hardest things students accomplish all year and should be celebrated accordingly.

- Publishing is an often-overlooked step, but this is how visual learners can make their writing even more expressive. These learners will see publishing and adding art as a reward for their hard work.

Publishing Reproducible

- The **Author Bio Form** reproducible (page 144) can go next to any published piece of writing or inside its cover. To inspire students, show them a few samples of author biographies on book covers or Web sites. Let them fill in the blanks and draw pictures of themselves in the space above their biographies. Cut out each Author Bio along the dashed lines.

Publishing Activities

- Art goes hand-in-hand with publishing. Each student can decorate a sheet of construction paper to make a booklet cover, displaying the title of the writing and her name on the front and the Author Bio on the back. For the text pages, students can simply decorate the edges of their papers or back them with construction paper to create frames before binding the booklets. They might like to write their final drafts in colored pencil or ink on the prepared pages.

- Allow each student to publish an illustration or photograph along with his writing. Some students might be interested in creating collages from magazine pictures instead of drawing. Use different visual ideas each time so that illustrating a story does not become routine.

- Students do not need to decorate their papers in order to publish them. You might consider covering a bulletin board with brightly colored paper and giving the display a title like *Superstar Writing*. After all students have published at least one piece of writing, encourage them to post their published papers on the board. Lead the class in clapping as each student pins up her paper.

- Invite students to make publishing a performance. Let each student choose one piece to read to the group. Limit readings to two or three students a day and spread out the readings over several days. Or, select a few students each day to read their works to a younger class.

- Students can store their best written work in special portfolios. Ask parents to help you provide colorful pocket folders. The disadvantage of using portfolios is that they take up valuable classroom space, but parents love to see the progress in their children's writing.

- If you can post your students' pieces of writing around the room or store them in portfolios, invite families for an authors' night. Provide refreshments and let students show off their work. Create several stations, such as:
  - ► Set up a listening/viewing station where parents can wear headphones and hear students read their writing or watch them read their works aloud.
  - ► Set out some final copies of student writing along with art supplies. Let students and their parents decorate publishable copies of their work.
  - ► Design a scenery backdrop using butcher paper and art supplies. Post it on the wall in a corner and let students act out their stories for parents.

- Many students will see working on the computer as a treat. Let them type their best written pieces on it. Help them experiment with fonts and colors. Post the typed papers in the classroom.

- Record students as they read their written work aloud. Put the recorded stories at a listening center for others to listen to.

Publishing Assignments

- **Language Arts**: Bind student stories together inside of cardboard covers to make a collection. Then, give your collection a title, such as *Stories by Mrs. Whitley's Class*. Store the book in the classroom library so that student writing has equal status with children's literature.

- **Math:** If you have students writing word problems, create worksheets from their best problems. Or, number the problems and post them around the room. Let students number their papers, walk around, and answer the problems.

- **Social Studies:** Have students prepare a class study guide for a social studies unit. For example, if you are teaching about types of houses, let each student draw a picture of a specific kind of house and write a paragraph to describe it. Sort pictures of similar houses together and then bind all of the pages to make a book. You may want to make a few copies of the pages before binding sets of them. Send the copies home with different students each night to help them learn the information.

Evaluation Ideas

Unless you are evaluating a finished product like a social studies project, a book report, or other type of report, publishing can be purely celebratory. If possible, give out grades for most writing before the publishing stage and let students use publishing as a reward for their hard work.

See directions on page 142.

_____ is
_____ is in
_____'s class at _____
_____ lives in _____.
_____ .
_____ .
with _____ likes
In spare time, _____
_____ .

_____ is
_____ is in
_____'s class at _____
_____ lives in _____.
_____ .
_____ .
with _____ likes
In spare time, _____
_____ .

Writing Test Ahead

Students may not face a writing element on a standardized test until third grade or later, but the work they do in early elementary school will help prepare them for responding to writing prompts at testing time. Regardless of what type of prompt students face on a test, you can be sure that the test graders will look for many of the things addressed in this book: a main idea, supporting details, a good conclusion, and adherence to conventions. If you work with students to help them master all of these elements in many different kinds of writing situations, hopefully, they will apply their knowledge to any kind of writing test prompt.

Special Tips for Writing Tests

- Teach students the vocabulary that will help them know how to approach different prompts. Writing test prompts can ask students to write a narrative (story), descriptive essay, persuasive essay, and directions. An understanding of the words *introduction*, *support* or *evidence* or *details*, *conclusion*, and *conventions* is important. Also, students should know that the phrase "respond to a prompt" means to write about it.

- During some class writing periods for those students who can handle the challenge, create a testing atmosphere and ask them to respond in writing to a prompt. Preparing them for the quiet environment and the rules and restrictions will help them be less nervous at test time.

- Good writers can be tripped up if they do not understand the prompts they are reading. To check comprehension, read prompts with students and ask them questions about how they think they should respond. Do extra reading and responding practice sessions with students with special needs and students whose second language is English.

Writing Tests Reproducible

- Introduce different kinds of writing prompts before using the **What Writing Prompt Is This?** reproducible. Help students learn the vocabulary they need for understanding writing prompts. Before completing this activity independently or with a partner, students should be able to identify whether they will be writing to tell a story, summarizing an article, or explaining something. Alternatively, you may wish to use this reproducible as a discussion tool.

As a first step to prepare students for future writing tests, encourage them to verbalize certain terms during class discussions and when working on writing tasks.

Writing Tests Activities

- Post different examples of the types of writing around the room, read them, and let students guess the genre of prompt for each. If you have students respond to any of the prompts, choose those that match the kind of prompt on your state's writing test.

- Some states' writing tests instruct students to respond to a story, usually by summarizing. Introduce short stories and expository pieces and summarize them as a class. Also, revisit the summarizing lessons in Chapter 3: Topic Talk and Chapter 9: Expository Expo.

- Students are sometimes asked to respond to pictures, usually by writing a story that includes them. After school one day, turn your classroom into an art gallery. Post prints from famous artists, local artists (art expo and local event posters will usually work), print ads, and even student art. Write the following instructions on the board or copy them on a handout for the students. *Choose a piece of artwork. Answer these questions about the art: What do you see in this picture? What do you think is happening? What do you think happened leading up to the picture? What will happen next?* Respond to student writing by praising and offering suggestions for improvement.

- Research the writing test given at your school and help those students who are capable writers plan how they use their time. For example, if students who are ready for this challenge are given 50 minutes to respond to a prompt, help them do 10 minutes of planning, brainstorming and prewriting, 20 minutes of writing, 10 minutes of revising and editing, and 10 minutes of writing their final drafts. As students respond to sample prompts, set a timer to go off at the end of each allotted time period. Eventually, students will learn to adjust the time they take to do each step of the writing process to match the timer.

Evaluation Ideas

Look for how well students handled the prompt, how well they were able to incorporate the brainstormed information, how correct their papers are, and how much time they used. As you give students more assignments to prepare them for prompts, keep the old ones on file so that you can look for arcs of improvement. Be sure to point out when a student is improving.

Name

What Writing Prompt Is This?

Work with a partner. Read each prompt. In each box, write the letter for what kind of prompt you think it is. Use the Word Bank.

Prompt 1: Read the article about dolphins and sharks. Write a paragraph that tells what the article is about. Include the most important details.

Prompt 2: It is near the end of the school year. Soon, you will be in the next grade. Write a letter to a student who is a year younger than you. Tell the student what to do to be a good student in your grade.

Prompt 3: Imagine that you wake up one morning and you have grown wings. Write a story about your new wings.

Prompt 4: Think about what you do every school day morning. Write a paragraph that tells what you do every day to get ready for school.

Prompt 5: Look at the picture of a forest. Imagine you are in this forest. Write a paragraph that describes what it is like to be in the forest.

Word Bank

A. descriptive

B. summary

C. expository

D. persuasive

E. narrative

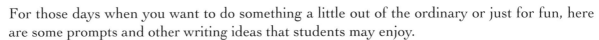
For those days when you want to do something a little out of the ordinary or just for fun, here are some prompts and other writing ideas that students may enjoy.

▶ Students choose descriptive words while building their fantasy playgrounds using the **Amazing Playground** reproducible (page 151). First, have students read the word bank and underline those words that best describe their imaginary playgrounds. Next, encourage students to draw pictures of their playgrounds. Finally, have each student write a paragraph about it.

▶ Let students generate ideas for designing a fun tree house. Distribute copies of **The Tree House** reproducible (page 152) and have students complete the activity by following the directions above for the Amazing Playground.

▶ Use the **Lost Dog Ad** (page 153) to combine description with art and story writing. Purchase a dog magazine. Let each student cut out a picture of a different dog to glue on the paper or have him draw a picture of a dog on it. To complete their activity sheets, students should fill in the blanks with descriptive words that match their pictures. Before you collect the completed ads, have students cut apart the pictures and the descriptions. After students leave for the day, post the dog pictures around the room. The next morning as students arrive, randomly distribute the descriptions and see whether every student can find the matching picture of a dog. Finally, have each student write a story about how the dog whose picture he looked for was found and happily reunited with its owner.

▶ Beef up your classroom library. Brainstorm crazy titles for books with students. To get them started, give some examples like *The Story of Marlon and the Bowl of Wiggly Gray Spaghetti* or *The Day I Let All of the Zoo Animals Out of Their Cages!* Then, let each student choose a title from the generated list and write a crazy story to go with it. Make a small book for each student by folding several sheets of paper in half and stapling them together. Guide students as they distribute the text from their stories over a few pages. They can also add illustrations to the pages to complete their books.

- On the whiteboard, write everyone's name in the class in alphabetical order. Help students generate rhyming words for each name. (Do not allow any rhymes that are likely to spawn hurtful nicknames.) Work together as a class to compose a silly song or poem that uses each student's name and its rhyme. For example, your poem could start off like this: *My name is Anna, and I love bananas!* or *My name is Casey, and I went to outer spacey!*

- Spend a few minutes with the class playing a game of Telephone but incorporate writing. First, play the game the usual way by whispering a few sentences to a chosen student and then having that student whisper the message to a classmate. The game continues until the last student announces what she heard to the class. Usually, the end message is very different from the beginning message. Play the game again; however, this time do the writing version. Each student should write down what they hear and then whisper it to the next classmate. Begin the activity by whispering a different message to the first student. She can jot down notes or record the complete message. Without showing her classmate what she wrote, have her whisper the message to the next student as she refers to her notes. Invite the final classmate in the message chain to read his writing aloud. Ask students what they think the benefit of writing messages is.

- Write a story as a class, one sentence at a time. Agree on the names of two characters beforehand and also whether they are people or animals. Write this agreement on the board. For example, you may write something like *Our two characters are a girl hippo named Francine and a boy hippo named Mike.* At the top of a sheet of paper, write the beginning of a story, such as *Francine and Mike were tired of living at the zoo,* and give it to a student. The chosen student adds one sentence to the story and then folds over the paper to cover your sentence but leaves hers showing. The paper is then passed on to the next student. Continue in this manner by having each student add a sentence and fold over the paper to cover all sentences but her own. Collect the story at the end and read it aloud to the class. Everyone will enjoy hearing the crazy story!

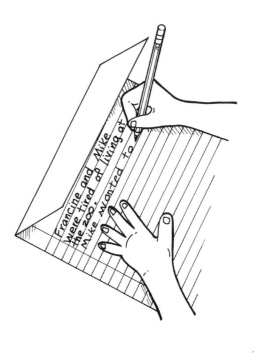

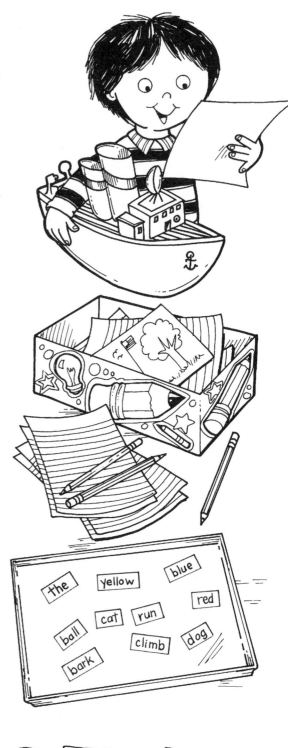

- Use show-and-tell as a jumping-off point for writing. Select several students to bring in items to share. Have students write short descriptive paragraphs about what they brought in and why they chose the items. Then, ask each student to read his piece of writing when it is his turn to show the item.

- Demonstrate how much students have learned about writing by making a class time capsule. At the beginning of the year, direct each student to draw a picture of anything she likes and then describe the picture by writing a few sentences on a separate sheet of paper. Store these materials until near the end of the school year. Redistribute the pictures and again, ask students to write about them. Do not show them their old pieces of writings until after they are finished. Then, let students compare the two paragraphs. Chances are the second writing samples will show a big improvement over the first.

- This fun writing activity makes a great display for a parent's night! Purchase a children's magnetic poetry kit or buy a regular kit and remove any objectionable words. Stick the magnets to a baking sheet. Store the baking sheet on a whiteboard tray or in a center and let students use it for word choice inspiration. To make this an interactive activity, let each student tape his writing paper onto the back of another baking sheet and write a story. When he gets to a point in a sentence where he wants to use one of the words, instead of writing it, let him stick the magnet to the baking sheet through the paper. Photograph their writings, so that students can place copies of their work in their portfolios.

- Create your own word-insert kit like the one above but without magnets. Have students cut out words from magazines. Label a set of zippered plastic bags with the parts of speech and sort the cutout words into the bags. Let students draw one word from each bag and write a story or paragraph using all of their selected words. They can glue or tape each word in place in their stories the first time they use it.

Amazing Playground

Imagine that you can build an amazing playground. It can have anything you want. Here are some words that could describe your playground.

blue	fast	new	short	sunny
bouncy	fun	red	slippery	super
curvy	funny	rough	smooth	tall
dark	green	sandy	soft	terrific
easy	hard	shady	speedy	wet
exciting	long	shiny	splashy	yellow

- Draw a line under each word above that you like.
- Draw a picture of your playground below.
- On another sheet of paper, write a story to tell about your playground. Try to use some of the words you underlined above.
- Write your own title for the story.

The Tree House

Imagine that you and a friend decide to build a fantastic tree house. It can have several rooms in a very large tree. What does your tree house look like? What can you see when you are in it? Here are some words that you can use.

beautiful	cool	hard	quiet	sturdy	thin
blue	distant	high	red	sunny	warm
billowy	easy	long	rough	super	wet
bright	exciting	new	shady	tall	white
calm	flying	orange	shiny	terrific	windy
chirping	green	purple	smooth	thick	yellow

- Draw a line under each word above that you like.
- Draw a picture of your tree house below.
- On another sheet of paper, write a story to tell about your tree house. Try to use some of the words you underlined above.
- Write your own title for the story.

Lost Dog Ad

Your dog is missing! You need to write an ad to put in the newspaper so that you can find your dog. Draw or glue a picture of your dog in the box.

Have you seen this dog?

_____ was lost on _____.

It is a _____. It has

_____, _____ fur. The dog has

_____ ears and a _____ tail.

The dog is about _____ _____ tall and weighs _____

_____. If you find this dog, please call _____

at _____. Thank you for your help.

Answer Key

Chapter 1: First Writing

Pages 19–27 (Decorative Blank List, Journal Page, ABC Journal, My Journal Page, Write-On Plate, You're invited . . . , Comment Card, Camp Windy Woods Application)
Answers will vary.

Chapter 2: Superb Sentences

Page 32 — Choosing Better Words
Part A
good — excellent, terrific
bad — terrible, horrible
happy — joyful, thrilled
sad — upset, miserable

Part B
pretty — lovely, beautiful
nice — gentle, kindly
ugly — homely, hideous
tired — exhausted, sleepy

Page 33–39 (Banking Some Words, Describe It! Writing Interesting Sentences)
Answers will vary.

Page 40 — Missing Capital Letters
Part A
1. Mom, After, I, Bert's
2. This, Austin, John, Bella, I, Sam, Megan, Nate
3. I, Dad
4. We, Smith

Part B
1. Today, Big Pond Road, We, Al's Pet Food Supply
2. In, Sunnyville, I, Main Street
3. Will, David
4. Let's, High Hills Park, Mark, Chen, Sora

Page 41 — Missing Capital Letters
Part C
1. My, Ava, Her, Lance, Ty, Colin
2. Wait, Jorge, Marta, Marta, I
3. Jenny, Spring Hills
4. We, Wiggle Worm Bait Shop, Dad, Jen, I

Part D
1. On, Sunday, Grandma's, Grandma
2. Tywan's, January, He
3. I, May, I, Walker Library, Saturday
4. My, Thomas, Percy, I, Henry

Page 42 — Please Punctuate
Part A
1. Can you come over for dinner? We are having tacos.
2. My favorite food is pizza. What foods do you like?
3. Would you like a snack? I can make it.
4. Please melt the cheese. I will put the chips on a dish.
5. Let's find the deck of cards. Which card game would you like to play?

Part B
1. Do not run into the street! I will get the ball for you.
2. Tomorrow is Hat Day at school. I will wear my baseball cap.
3. Did you know that Cam got chicken pox? He feels better now.
4. Max just hit a home run! He is a good hitter.
5. Surprise, Ally! We are happy to see you.

Page 43 — You Be the Editor! Part A
Note: Corrections are in boldfaced type.
Can you guess what **I** did this summer**?** My Aunt **Liz** and Uncle Jon own a camp. It is on Lake **James.** It is called Camp Canyonlands. Last **August**, I was finally old enough to go**.** I stayed in a cabin with five other boys. Their names were Ian, Caleb, John, Andre, and Evan. My bunk was over Ian's bunk. It was next to John's bunk. The first night, we all wrote letters. I wrote to my sister **Katie**. The other boys were a little homesick. My aunt and uncle came to see me, so I was not sad. They brought us cookies. **In** the morning, Ian helped me make my bed. I helped **John** make his bed. **We** all sat together at breakfast. We played basketball. We went swimming in **Lake James**. After lunch, we rode horses. My horse was named **Snowball**. What color do you think she was**?** She was a black horse! We had a campfire at dinner. **We** toasted hot dogs and marshmallows. We were very tired and went to sleep fast**.** My first day of camp was great**!**

Page 44 — You Be the Editor! Part B
Note: Corrections are in boldfaced type.
I go to **Midlands** School. Today, I am staying home**.**
It is a snow day. **It** is the sixth snow day we have had
in **January**. It is freezing outside! **Mom** says we are
going to make ice skaters today. **First**, she put a pan
of water in the freezer**.** Next, she gave me a clothespin.
I drew eyes and a face on it**.** I named my skater
Lily**.** Mom filled a paper cup with water. We put the
clothespin in the cup. Mom put it in the freezer**.** **When**
we took it out later, can you guess what happened**?**
It froze**!** I peeled off the cup. There was a block of ice
around the clothespin. **Mom** took out the pan of ice.
Now, my skater **Lily** can slide across her very own ice
rink. I can't wait to show my friend Nora. **Mom** said
I can help **Nora** make her own skater**.** Then, we can
play together. Do you think there will be a snow day
tomorrow**?** I hope so**!**

Page 45 — Commas Needed
Note: Corrections are in boldfaced type.
Part A
1. I looked for my bat**,** baseball**,** and glove.
2. Mom drove Makayla**,** Mitch**,** and me to the ball
   field.
3. My team wore red**,** white**,** and black shirts.
4. We ate popcorn**,** peanuts**,** and watermelon after the
   game.
5. There are ball games on Tuesday**,** Thursday**,** and
   Saturday.

Part B
1. Before we left the house**,** we had to put away our
   toys.
2. After driving to the park**,** we ran from the car to the
   pool.
3. Everyone is ready to swim**,** but I forgot my towel.
4. I left my towel in the car**,** so I ran back to get it.
5. The sunshine is hot**,** so my mom is sitting in the
   shade.

Page 46 — Come On, Commas!
Note: Corrections are in boldfaced type.
1. On my friend Tom's birthday**,** I was making a cake.
2. I went to the store to buy butter**,** eggs**,** and milk.
3. After making the cake**,** I made the icing.
4. Tom**,** Drew**,** and Beth were waiting for me at the
   party.
5. It was time for me to leave**,** so I got a box to put the
   cake in.
6. Since I needed to hurry**,** I rushed out the door.
7. I tripped on the step**,** fell down**,** and dropped the box!
8. When the box fell open**,** I saw that it was empty.

9. I had put in the cake plate**,** but I forgot to put in the cake.
10. When I got to the party**,** I was late. Everyone liked
    my cake.

Page 47 — Prepositions on the Page
Words circled:
Row 1 — under, with; Row 2 — over, near
Row 3 — inside, beside; Row 4 — around, by
Row 5 — to, at
Completed sentences:
1. The skunk sprayed my dog in the face.
2. My friend parked her scooter next to mine.
3. Our team played soccer on the field.
4. We had to put the blocks in the bin.
5. The horse jumped over the fence.
6. I climbed up the ladder.

Page 48 — Add a Prepositional Phrase
Answers will vary.

Page 49 — Sentence Combo Part A
Answers may vary slightly from these.
1. Katie ate lunch and then went outside.
2. Dean plays the piano and the drums.
3. Fred took a bath but did not brush his teeth.

Page 50 — Sentence Combo Part B
Answers may vary slightly from these.
1. I want to play outside, but it is raining.
2. The geese swam in the pond with the goslings.
3. Jamel ran to the park and then slid down the slide.

Chapter 3: Topic Talk

Page 54 — Main Idea Pictures Part A
Picture 1: Two children are playing with a Frisbee and
          a dog is trying to play, too.
Picture 2: An owl is trying to catch a mouse.

Page 55 — Main Idea Pictures Part B
Picture 1: The alien on the bicycle is waving to another
          alien on a scooter.
Picture 2: A child is choosing a prize at the dentist's
          office.

Page 56 — Topic Finders Part A
Story A: A surprise trip
Story B: Hurricanes

Page 57 — Topic Finders Part B
Story A: New pets
Story B: Visiting Nana

Page 58—Topic Match
Topic: Frogs are very interesting animals.
They grow legs and lose their tails.
They are so loud when they croak at night!
The tadpoles look like tiny fish.
The adults catch bugs with their sticky tongues.

Topic: I liked being the catcher at baseball practice.
My coach showed me how to pull off the mask and catch a foul ball.
This was my first time behind home plate.
I threw a ball all the way to second base.
The catcher's gear was heavy.

Topic: The pink pants my mom bought for me are very cool!
I had to go shopping for a new pair of pants.
I like the stars sewn on the pockets.
Pink is my very favorite color.
I can wear them with my new pink tennis shoes.

Chapter 4: Prewriting with a Purpose

Pages 63—66
Answers will vary.

Chapter 5: Stopping for Directions

Page 70—Looking for Clues That Show Order Part A
Words circled: Sunday, end, Then, third, After, last, when, fourth

Page 71—Looking for Clues That Show Order Part B
Words circled: after, First, Second, Third, Later, Last, Next

Page 72—Looking for Clues That Show Order C
Words circled: while, First, soon, Then, ten days, Finally, Now, Tomorrow

Page 73—Directions in Order Part A
1–This is how I make a banana split.
6–Mom helps me scoop ice cream on top of the banana.
4–I ask my mom to cut the banana in half.
3–Next, I get out some ice cream, whipped cream, and a banana.
5–I put the banana halves into the dish.
2–First, I get a dish out of the cabinet.
7–Then, I squirt whipped cream on top of the ice cream. Yum!

Page 73—Directions in Order Part B
1–This is how to get to the mall from my house.
6–Turn right onto Oak Road.
3–Ride east on Maple Way and turn south onto Elm Street.
2–Turn right out of the driveway of my house onto Maple Way.
7–Take the first exit from Oak Road into the Tree Branch Mall parking lot.
5–Take Holly Lane until you reach Oak Road.
4–From Elm Street, turn east onto Holly Lane.

Pages 75—78 (Recipe Card Template, Getting Around at School, I Am an Expert! Science Steps)
Answers will vary.

Chapter 6: Paragraph Power

Pages 83—85 Underlining Paragraph Parts A, B & C
In all three paragraphs, the first sentence should be underlined in green. Each last sentence should be underlined in red. All other sentences should be underlined in blue. Titles will vary.

Page 86—Topic Sentence Match Part A
Story A: You never know what you will find under a rock.
Story B: This is a fun way to play with dominoes.

Page 87—Topic Sentence Match Part B
Story A: There are many different fish to see at the zoo.
Story B: The water-holding frog is a very unusual frog.

Page 88—Body Sentence Sort
Topic Sentence: Look out for fish that spit!
Detail Sentences: Archerfish like to eat insects. They look for food on plants that are near the water. When they find food, they swim under it. They stick their mouths out of the water. The fish aims its tongue at the insect. Then, it spits water into the air. When the water hits the insect, it falls in. The fish eats it.

Topic Sentence: It can be hard to find a good place to look at the night sky with a telescope.
Detail Sentences: Find a place where trees will not block the sky. Try to stand on a deck or climb a hill. It also helps to find a dark place. Do not stand under a streetlight. Since it will be dark, stand in a safe place. Do not stand near a street or where you can fall. When you find a good spot on a clear night, you will be able to see the moon, many stars, and some planets. Finding a perfect spot for your telescope will be worth it.

Page 90—Misfit Sentences Part A
Sentences crossed out in red:
Story A: I like to wear a coat when it is cold.
Story B: Rabbits have fluffy tails.

Page 91—Misfit Sentences Part B
Sentences crossed out in red:
Story A: They live in groups called *mobs*.
Story B: I like to be outside on a sunny day.

Pages 92 and 93—Write the Body Parts A and B
Answers will vary.

Page 94—Choose the Best Ending
Story A: We are excited to see our families and eat ice cream at school.
Story B: The New Year is fun around the world.

Page 95–98 (Write the Ending, Paragraph in Training)
Answers will vary.

Page 99—Mixed-Up Message Part A
Answers may vary slightly. Accept any order that makes sense.

Today in class, we played a game called Musical Chairs. First, we put all of our chairs in a circle. Next, the music teacher took away one chair. The music teacher started the music. We all walked around the chairs while the music was on. When the music stopped, we each tried to sit in a chair. My friend Sam did not get a chair, so he was out. The teacher took away another chair. Since Sam was out, he got to start the music. We walked around the chairs again. Sam stopped the music. I could not find a chair! I was out, too! At least I get to start and stop the music next time.

Page 100—Mixed-Up Message Part B
Answers may vary slightly. Accept any order that makes sense.

My favorite game is Seven Up. Seven people stand in front of the class. They are the tappers. The rest of us sit at our desks. We put our heads down and hide our eyes. With our eyes shut, we stick out our thumbs. Each tapper walks around and taps one person on the thumb. Everyone whose thumb is tapped puts his thumb down. When the tappers finish tapping, they go back to the front of the room. We try to guess who tapped our thumbs. If someone guesses wrong, the tapper stays up front. If someone guesses right, she gets to trade places with tapper. We play the game until the teacher says it is time to stop.

Page 101—Mixed-Up Message Part C
Answers may vary slightly. Accept any order that makes sense.

My sister Anna loves to play Duck, Duck, Goose. She and her friends sit in a circle. One person gets to be "It." "It" walks around the circle. "It" taps each player on the head. He says, "Duck," every time he taps someone. When he says, "Goose," that person has to chase him around the circle and tries to tag him. If the Goose catches "It," "It" must sit in the middle of the circle for the next game. Then, the Goose gets to be the new "It." If the Goose cannot catch"It," the Goose sits in the middle for the next game. Then, the same person is "It" again. You can see why this game is exciting!

Chapter 7: Strong Stories

Page 108—Using Your Five Senses
Answers will vary.

Page 109—Seek Out the Senses Part A
Underline in blue: cloudy
Underline in green: hear her call out, rattling, noisy car
(Students may also underline dialogue.)
Underline in yellow: cool and damp, big hugs, face itches, scratchy sweater
Underline in orange: smells like coal and cars
Underline in red: tastes very rich

Page 110—Seek Out the Senses Part B
Underline in blue: dark, bright
Underline in green: heard the bell ring, hear their tongues lapping, Miss Ollie said, She said
Underline in yellow: cold (twice), cold metal, warm and soft
Underline in orange: smelled spicy
Underline in red: very sweet

Page 111—Where Am I? Part A
Story A: Underwater in the ocean (water in ears, blowing bubbles, hair floated around her head, fish nearby, a ray swam under me)
Story B: A movie theater (sticky floor, dark, hot popcorn, smelled like butter, fuzzy seats, middle of a row, loud music, lights came up)

Page 112—Where Am I? Part B
Story A: In a car in the swimming pool parking lot (hot pavement, car is hot, damp towel, wet hair, red eyes, hear people splashing and sliding)
Story B: The waiting room of a dentist's office (funny smell, buzzing, sound of water, waiting, read a magazine, little rooms, climbed into the chair, bright lights, open mouth)

Page 113—Character Hunt
Character #1: Mia
Character #2: Matt
Character #3: Mia and Matt's mom
Character #4: Umi-001

Pages 114 and 115—Name the Characters
Answers will vary. All #1s should match, all #2s should match, all #3s should match, and all #4s should match.

Page 116—Character Planner
Answers will vary.

Page 117—Silly Faces
Answers will vary.

Page 118—Who Said What?
Quotation marks are in boldfaced type.
Witt and Poppy wanted to play a game.
"I want to play checkers,**"** said Witt.
"We don't have a checkerboard,**"** replied Poppy.
"Can we play baseball?**"** asked Witt hopefully.
"I don't have a bat,**"** said Poppy. **"**Maybe we could jump rope.**"**
"Jumping rope is not very fun,**"** sighed Witt.
"Wait a minute!**"** shouted Poppy. She ran into her bedroom. She came back with two rackets.
"What are those for?**"** asked Witt.
"Let's go down to the park and play tennis!**"** said Poppy excitedly.
"Do you have tennis balls?**"** asked Witt.
"No, I guess not. Sorry,**"** said Poppy sadly.
"My brother has some,**"** said Witt. **"**Let me run to my house and get them!**"**
"I will meet you in my front yard,**"** said Poppy.

Pages 119–125 (Picture Problems, Solve the Problem, Writing a Good Conclusion, Planning Your Story, Check Your Setting, What's the Problem? Whose Story Is This?)
Answers will vary.

Chapter 8: Passing Notes (and Letters and E-mail)

Page 128—Friendly Letter Template
Answers will vary.

Chapter 9: Expository Expo

Page 131—Book Review Form
Answers will vary.

Chapter 10: Revising with Relish

Pages 134–136 (Make Your Paragraph Better, Make Your Story Better, Help Your Friend Revise)
Answers will vary.

Chapter 11: Convening with Conventions

Page 139—Editing Checklist
Answers will vary.

Page 141—Editing Treasure Hunt
Answers will vary.

Chapter 12: Proud to Be Published

Page 144—Author Bio Form
Answers will vary.

Chapter 13: Writing Test Ahead

Page 147—What Writing Prompt Is This?
Prompt 1: B. summary
Prompt 2: D. persuasive
Prompt 3: E. narrative
Prompt 4: C. expository
Prompt 5: A. descriptive

Chapter 14: Extra-Fun Extras

Pages 151–153 (Amazing Playground, The Tree House, Lost Dog Ad)
Answers will vary.

Correlations to Standards

Make Writing Exciting! supports the following recommendations from the National Council of Teachers of English (NCTE) and International Reading Association (IRA) *Standards for the English Language Arts* and the teaching practices outlined in *Learning to Read and Write: Developmentally Appropriate Practices for Young Children*, a position statement of the National Association for the Education of Young Children (NAEYC) and the International Reading Association. This resource also supports the National Council of Teachers of Mathematics (NCTM) *Principles and Standards for School Mathematics*, the *National Science Education Standards*, and the National Council for the Social Studies (NCSS) *Curriculum Standards for Social Studies*.

NCTE/IRA *Standards for the English Language Arts*

This book supports the following standards:

1. **Students read many different types of print and nonprint texts for a variety of purposes.**
   Students read certain sentences, longer texts, and pictures while doing the activities.

2. **Students read literature from various time periods, cultures, and genres in order to form an understanding of humanity.**
   Many of the activities in this book are based on literature that either the student has read or the teacher has read to them.

3. **Students use a variety of strategies to build meaning while reading.**
   Make Writing Exciting! introduces and reinforces a wide range of literacy concepts, skills, and strategies, including sequencing, vocabulary development, identifying main ideas and details, and summarizing.

4. **Students communicate in spoken, written, and visual form, for a variety of purposes and a variety of audiences.**
   Even though this book focuses primarily on written communication, students also do a great deal of verbal communication through discussions and visual communication through illustrations while completing the suggested writing activities.

5. **Students use the writing process to write for different purposes and different audiences.**
   Make Writing Exciting! provides activities for all stages of the writing process and for a wide variety of writing genres.

6. **Students incorporate knowledge of language conventions (grammar, spelling, punctuation), media techniques, and genres to create and discuss a variety of print and nonprint texts.**
   Activities on editing and publishing, along with a focus on different types of writing, support this

standard. Students learn to both write and talk about writing through the suggested activities.

7. **Students conduct research on a variety of topics and present their research findings in ways appropriate to their purpose and audience.**
   Certain writing activities in *Make Writing Exciting!* incorporate research.

8. **Students use technology and media resources such as libraries, databases, computer networks, and video to collect information and to communicate.**
   The use of technology and different media to produce writing is encouraged in this book.

9. **Students become participating members of a variety of literacy communities.**
   The whole- and small-group activities throughout *Make Writing Exciting!* help teachers build a classroom literacy community.

10. **Students use spoken, written, and visual language for their own purposes, such as to learn, for enjoyment, or to share information.**
    With a focus on both informal and formal writing, the resource helps students improve their writing for different purposes and in different contexts.

NAEYC/IRA Position Statement *Learning to Read and Write: Developmentally Appropriate Practices for Young Children*

This book supports the following recommended teaching practices for primary-grade students:

1. **Teachers read to children daily and provide opportunities for students to independently read both fiction and nonfiction texts.**
   Make Writing Exciting! includes many activities that start with the teacher reading to students or students reading texts themselves.

2. **Teachers provide opportunities for students to write many different kinds of texts for different purposes.**
   Make Writing Exciting! teaches a wide variety of writing types, from informal to formal.

3. **Teachers provide writing experiences that allow children to develop from the use of nonconventional writing forms to more conventional forms.**
   Make Writing Exciting! helps students move from writing informal items like lists and notes to more formal items like paragraphs and stories. In addition, many activities allow for drawing, "driting," and dictation if these techniques better meet a student's current needs.

4. **Teachers provide opportunities for children to work in small groups.**
   There are several suggested small-group activity ideas.

5. **Teachers provide challenging instruction that expands children's vocabularies.**
   The word-choice exercises and many other activities in *Make Writing Exciting!* help students build their vocabularies.

6. **Teachers adapt teaching strategies based on the individual needs of a child.**
   To meet individual student needs, *Make Writing Exciting!* presents many ways to modify activities, including the use of drawing, "driting," and dictation.

NCTM *Principles and Standards for School Mathematics*

Select activities support the following Number and Operations Standard Expectations for Grades Pre-K–2:

1. **Students understand the meanings of addition and subtraction of whole numbers and how the two operations relate to each other.**
   The Math Cross-Curricular Sentence Assignment supports this standard.

2. **Students understand what happens when they add or subtract whole numbers.**
   The Math Cross-Curricular Sentence Assignment supports this standard.

One activity supports the following Geometry Standard Expectation for Grades Pre-K–2:

1. **Students identify, create, draw, compare, and sort two- and three-dimensional shapes.**
   One of the Math Cross-Curricular List Assignments supports this standard.

National Science Education Standards

Certain activities support the following Science as Inquiry Standard for Grades K–4:

1. **All students should develop the ability to do scientific inquiry.**
   Several of the Science Cross-Curricular Assignments that deal with writing scientific procedures and observations support this standard.

Select activities support the following Life Science Standard for Grades K–4:

1. **All students should understand the characteristics of organisms.**
   The Science Cross-Curricular Assignments for Lists and Information and Reports support this standard.

Certain activities support the following Science in Personal and Social Perspectives Standard for Grades K–4:

1. **All students should develop understanding of personal health.**
   Several Science Cross-Curricular Assignments support this standard.

NCSS *Curriculum Standards for Social Studies*

Select activities support the following performance expectations for students in the early grades:

People, Places & Environments
1. **Students create and use mental maps of different areas that show their understanding of location, direction, size, and shape.**
   The Social Studies Cross-Curricular Directions Assignment supports this expectation.

Production, Distribution & Consumption
1. **Students describe how price relates to supply and demand.**
   One of the Social Studies Cross-Curricular List Assignments supports this expectation.